How to Evaluate Your Christian Education Program

Books by D. Campbell Wyckoff
Published by The Westminster Press

HOW TO EVALUATE YOUR CHRISTIAN EDUCATION PROGRAM

THEORY AND DESIGN OF CHRISTIAN EDUCATION CURRICULUM

THE GOSPEL AND CHRISTIAN EDUCATION

THE TASK OF CHRISTIAN EDUCATION

The Cooperative Series
This book has been developed through the cooperative efforts of many denominations seeking through an interdenominational agency, the Cooperative Publication Association, to provide publications of sound educational values and practical usefulness.

How to Evaluate
Your Christian Education Program

by D. CAMPBELL WYCKOFF

Published for
THE COOPERATIVE PUBLICATION ASSOCIATION
by
THE WESTMINSTER PRESS, PHILADELPHIA

Library of Congress Catalog Card No. 62-8080

PRINTED IN THE UNITED STATES OF AMERICA

PREFACE

How to Evaluate Your Christian Education Program was developed at the request of the Committee on Administration and Leadership of the Division of Christian Education of the National Council of the Churches of Christ in the United States of America. Former bulletins on church school standards needed to be replaced with a new document that would reflect a broader concept of Christian education and a more flexible approach to standards.

After the basic document was approved in principle by the committee in October, 1959, it was carefully scrutinized by a group of research, field, and publishing people for its method of gathering data, its practicality, and its design. Revisions were made in the light of the suggestions of this group.

The revised document was then field-tested during the early months of 1960. About fifty churches participated. Detailed comments and criticisms were received from many of these churches, and most of the suggestions have been incorporated in this book. The document that was developed, field-tested, and revised in the manner just described appears in this book as Part Two, "A Plan for Local Parish Appraisal in Christian Education," and Part Three, "Forms." An introductory Part One has been prepared by the author to place the subject of evaluation in a larger context, including the appraisal of individual attainment. The book does not attempt, however, to provide a specific program and necessary forms for appraising individuals.

Although a few of the churches that tried out the plan found that it was not suitable to their needs, most found it helpful and useful. Many of those who were most successful in conducting the evaluation urged that others be told that using this plan will prove to be a rewarding experience for a church—if it is taken seriously, planned for carefully, interpreted thoroughly, given enough time, and led by really concerned and able people. Taken superficially, done hurriedly, and expected to work miracles, it is not likely to have very significant results.

D. C. W.

CONTENTS

PART THREE: FORMS

INTRODUCTION

Evaluation is a process of comparing what is with what ought to be, in order to determine areas and directions for improvement. The existing situation is first described and analyzed. Standards are set up by which to appraise the situation. The two are compared. Note is taken, as the comparison proceeds, of things that are weak, strong, omitted, and overemphasized. From these notations, implications for improvement are developed into a plan or strategy for the future.

Fundamentally, the process could not be simpler or more obvious: a comparison, from which implications are drawn. Yet the apparent simplicity of evaluation tends to disappear in the face of some of the complexities that arise at each step. How, for instance, shall we go about getting the facts on the existing situation? What categories shall we establish for collecting and organizing them? How may we be sure that they are truly the facts and that they add up to an accurate picture? Again, what standards shall we use? In what categories shall they be established? How shall they be validated? Comparison of facts with standards implies that the categories used in each case will match each other, again raising the question of adequate categories for analysis. How may we be confident that we have identified the really significant implications for improvement? How may we proceed to the formulation and acceptance of practical steps for improvement? Is there a way of assuring that these steps for improvement will be taken and that the improvements will be made?

Any practical-minded person will agree that the process of evaluation is useless unless each of these problems, right up to the last one, has been solved. The purpose of this book is to provide a guide to the process of evaluation in which all these questions have been faced forthrightly, so that a local parish may study its Christian education work with some assurance that it is not merely skimming the surface. The result, of course, is not a simple check list, nor a study in which a church finds its "score" in terms of standard norms set up outside, but rather the kind of study in which a parish is invited to look at itself and its work slowly, analytically, deeply, and in terms of its own problems, needs, and objectives. This, according to some who

9

have used preliminary forms of the study, is evaluation "the hard way," but it is well worth it.

A deep evaluation of a parish's Christian education program assumes that the standards for Christian education are rooted in basic conceptions of the objective of Christian education, curriculum principles, and principles of administration. These reflect and focus the practical concerns of Christian education in the parish.

The statement of the objective of Christian education is an attempt to state the purpose of the whole process, the answer to the questions "Why?" and "What for?" For purposes of evaluation, a basic objective is needed that will express briefly and clearly our understanding of the meaning of the process, our answer to the "Why?" and "What for?" and our most essential policies on the matter. In this guide, the objective formulated in the document *The Objective of Christian Education for Senior High Young People* (National Council of the Churches of Christ in the U.S.A., 1958) is used, partly because of its theological and educational adequacy, and partly because of its wide current use in Protestant circles:

> The objective of Christian education is to help persons to be aware of God's self-disclosure and seeking love in Jesus Christ and to respond in faith and love—to the end that they may know who they are and what their human situation means, grow as sons of God rooted in the Christian community, live in the Spirit of God in every relationship, fulfill their common discipleship in the world, and abide in the Christian hope.

The suggestion embodied in this guide is that parishes start their study of objective and standards by considering this statement and by revising or replacing it to meet their particular needs and position.

Since the curriculum is the church's systematic plan for Christian education, curriculum evaluation (both in terms of content and process) is in many ways the heart of the matter. If the basic standard is the objective, then curriculum standards are derived from the objective, in the sense of giving answers to curriculum questions that are in harmony with that objective. The curriculum questions are "Where?" (context), "What?" (scope), and "How?" (process, method, and design). This guide suggests that the parish consider and adapt for its own purposes such positions as these on context, scope, and process:

Context:

The context of Christian education is the worshiping, witnessing, and working community of persons in Christ.

10

Scope:

The scope of Christian education is the whole field of relationships (our experience of the divine, the human, nature, and history) in the light of the gospel.

Process:

The process, or method, of Christian education is participation in the life and work of the community of persons in Christ. (The design of the curriculum provides sequential and flexible forms for such participation.)

These are more fully delineated in the body of the guide, and are even more completely treated in the author's book *Theory and Design of Christian Education Curriculum* (The Westminster Press, 1961).

Administration is the means for implementing the curriculum. Planning, organization, management, and supervision are currently recognized as the ingredients in Christian education administration. The basic principle for this phase of the work is the principle of context: the administration of Christian education is either an integral expression of the nature and functioning of the worshiping, witnessing, working community of persons in Christ, or it is not true to its source, nature, and task. Planning, as a first step in administration, must be purposeful, a direct expression of the objective of Christian education in terms of a particular situation involving particular persons and groups. Organization is to be functional: there should be only such organization as is needed; new needs should bring new organization into existence; organization should be eliminated and radically modified as needs disappear or change. Management is to be democratic: authority and responsibility are to be placed in the hands of particular persons by consent of those involved; participation in decision-making is to have as broad a base as possible in the church; persons are to be trained in the roles of leader and participant. Supervision is to be co-operative: everyone (congregation, families, teachers, pupils, leaders, groups, officers, and the rest) is to be involved in discussing and setting standards, evaluating, making decisions regarding improvements, and carrying out these decisions.

Again, this study tries to embody in a concrete way this co-operative process of supervision as it relates to the whole gamut of administrative and curricular concerns. In seeking to do so, there are many aspects that may seem cumbersome, even though an attempt has been made to keep them at an absolute minimum. Perhaps it is too much to ask that such a study as this be efficient and co-operative at the same time! At least the attempt has been to combine the two qualities. If, however, one or the other has had to be sacrificed, the sacrifice has not been on the side of the co-operative principle.

Where objective, curriculum principles, and principles of administration are concerned, no doubt should exist in anyone's mind about the order or priority. Absolute priority goes to the objective, since it expresses the heart of the meaning of Christian education, theologically and educationally. The curriculum in turn implements the objective by providing a systematic plan for education. The administration consists of ways of implementing the curriculum in actual institutional forms. The order must never be reversed! Administrative concerns must never determine curriculum; curricular concerns must never determine the objective.

In this guide, standards are very specific forms of a fundamental principle. They are ways of showing what the principles mean in particular practical situations. Take, for instance, a standard such as this: "Each church school class at the senior high level shall meet in group session for study for a period of at least fifty minutes a week, except when individual assignments or group projects require their presence elsewhere." Such a statement is a standard because it gives a clear and unmistakable idea of what is to take place. Whether or not the standard is met may be easily ascertained in any particular situation. At the same time, such a standard is clearly related to the basic principle of process: "The process of Christian education is participation in the life and work of the community of persons in Christ." That life and work involve group study but may also involve other kinds of activities that should make the use of the group study period rather flexible in character.

This guide is primarily centered upon the problem of the evaluation of the institutions and programs of Christian education. The matter of evaluation of individual attainment must not be neglected, however. Chapter 1 deals with the theory, and to some extent the practice, of individual evaluation. There follows Chapter 2 on the theory of institutional evaluation. Part Two consists of a detailed plan for institutional evaluation.

Part One
THE PROCESS OF EVALUATION

1

APPRAISING INDIVIDUAL ATTAINMENT

THE APPRAISAL of individual attainment is constantly with us whether we plan for it or not. Most often it takes the form of personal subjective assessment. We ask ourselves: How did I do? Am I getting there? What am I good for? Has my life been worth living? Ever-present standardized hurdles loom in our pathway, many of them put there by the educational system that we have built: examinations, diplomas, degrees, and licenses. More and more we are taking to rating others systematically; we do it every time we fill out a reference blank. Personnel practices in business, education and the church depend to a great extent on the process of rating in this way. But as Christian educators our great concern, so far as the individual is concerned, is for personal results. Is our program of Christian education effective in terms of personal change and growth?

To raise the question of appraising individual attainment is to be beset by qualms, both theoretical qualms and technical qualms. Our theoretical qualms cluster about such questions as: How may we possibly understand the individual and his development, since they are essentially private and inaccessible, and since they are much more truly under God's care and direction than under ours? What criteria for evaluation shall be used? Criteria we must have, if we are going to evaluate at all, but where shall they come from, and what shall they be? Our technical qualms cluster about such questions as: How may reliable and valid data on the individual be gathered? How may these data be interpreted? How shall the findings be used?

Aspects of Individual Evaluation

In some communions, about all the individual evaluation that is done is in terms of catechizing, in order to determine worthiness for the rite of confirmation. In some others, the only individual evaluation that is attempted is in terms of testimony,

which is used as a basis for determining worthiness for admission to baptism. The use of catechizing and testimony in connection with admission to full communion indicates that individual evaluation is thrust upon us, whether we like it or not.

Some exploration has been undertaken in the use of paper-and-pencil tests in Christian education, but most of it was done during the 1920s and 1930s, and has not been continued. There were tests in the areas of Biblical and doctrinal knowledge, including the Laycock test and the Northwestern University tests. A recent attempt in this area is chronicled in the volume edited by Arthur L. Miller, *Tests and Measurements in Lutheran Education* (Lutheran Education Association, 1957). Tests were used to evaluate character, the most famous tests being those of Hartshorne and May. (See *Studies in the Nature of Character*, 3 vols.; The Macmillan Company, 1928, 1929, 1930.) At present, in the area of Christian character education, fairly sophisticated evaluation methods are being devised and used by Ernest M. Ligon and his associates in the Character Research Project, Union College, Schenectady, New York. (See Ernest M. Ligon, *Dimensions of Character;* The Macmillan Company, 1956.) Thurstone pioneered in the area of testing beliefs and attitudes; Ernest J. Chave's *Measure Religion* (University of Chicago Bookstore, 1939) was the outstanding example of this kind of testing. Some attempts have been made to test theological conceptualization, as in "Hearing the Word" (*Jr-Hi Notebook*, July-September, 1950. Board of Christian Education of the Presbyterian Church in the U.S.A.).

As lacking in permanency and influence as testing has been in Protestant education, it has raised several key questions. One such question is, What are we trying to evaluate? Are we trying to evaluate religious concepts (in which case paper-and-pencil tests and interviews would probably do perfectly well)? skills (in which case observation would be the key)? attitudes (in which case interviews or projective tests would probably be called for)? or habits (where longitudinal case studies might be required)?

Another question raised by the testing enterprise has been that of the objective involved. Say for the moment that we might be guided by an objective such as this: that God's will may be done in the lives of these learners. Whatever else is involved (and there are many other factors implied), a personal, inner, as well as corporate, process of theologizing is called for, since theology is reflection on God's will. Is such an inner and corporate process of theologizing, then, the core of the process of appraisal of individual attainment? If so, then testing is possible, for such a process is fairly accessible to view by oneself and by others. It is relatively public in character, or may easily be made so. Yet if other objectives are used, a more private and inaccessible process may well be involved, and testing may become very difficult or even totally inappropriate.

Outside of Christian education, in the field of general educational testing, vast developments have taken place in the testing of intelligence, ability, aptitude, interests, and achievement. The availability of electronic scoring devices has stepped up considerably the use and speed of testing in these fields. Projective techniques (those means by which a person rather unconsciously "gives himself away" by telling the story that a picture suggests to him, drawing a human figure, identifying meaningful shapes in ink blots, and the like) have been built into personality tests, most of which are interpreted in terms of modified psychiatric insights, and many of which are used by guidance workers in the schools. Daniel A. Prescott has summarized the educational uses of the case study in helping to individualize instruction in the schools in his book *The Child in the Educative Process* (McGraw-Hill Book Co., Inc., 1957). Prescott shows how testing may be used in the context of total understanding of the child through data of many kinds from a variety of sources. Educational research, testing, and measurement have been spurred on by professional groups such as the American Educational Research Association and the National Council on Measurements Used in Education.

The general field of evaluation has also seen key developments in the measurement of participation, from the simple matter of attendance records and their use to the delicate analysis of group dynamics. Emphasis has moved from participation as mere presence and quantity to the types and qualities of personal involvement in the processes of group exploration, problem solving, and learning.

The invention of "teaching machines" has also been a spur to evaluation in education, since evaluation at every point is built into the programming that is used in all such machines. The reinforcement theory in learning holds that a right response, if immediately rewarded, is likely to be learned in a permanent way. When a subject is programmed (arranged in logical and systematic learning steps) for a teaching machine, it is possible to evaluate at every step of the way, by indicating right and wrong responses. Thus there is no lag between the time of the response and the identification of it as right or wrong. The satisfaction of the right response produces the binding effect, while the indication of the wrong response will send the individual back to relearn the step before the wrong response has a chance to "set."

Evidences of new interest in Christian education evaluation, particularly of individual appraisal, are increasing. Various denominations (United Lutheran, Protestant Episcopal, Presbyterian U.S., and United Presbyterian U.S.A., among them) have established research offices that deal with this matter. The Bureau of Research and Survey of the National Council of the Churches of Christ in the U.S.A. has undertaken several studies that include concern for individual appraisal, and has sponsored an institute on evaluation in Christian education, held at Drew University, Madison, New Jersey, in September, 1959. (See *Evaluation and Christian Education;* National Council of the Churches of Christ in the U.S.A., 1960.) In the summer of 1961, the National Council of Churches sponsored a workshop on curriculum evaluation at Cornell University, Ithaca, New York. Immediately following, on the same campus, the Religious Education Association sponsored a workshop on research design.

Theory of Individual Evaluation

The essence of the process of evaluation may be put in the three steps that are by now familiar. First, set your standards. Second, describe your situation. Third, compare the two, appraising the situation in terms of the standard.

To be more analytical and more useful for individual appraisal, these three steps may be expanded to five.

1. Decide on categories for analysis. (These categories must be such that they break the total problem into bits that can be handled. They must also encompass the total problem, so that information gathered within them will add up to full information on the problem. They must be useful both as categories for standards and for description.)
2. Work out standards. (For each category, one or more standard is to be articulated, a standard being a statement that describes the way in which the category ought to be handled.)
3. Gather data. (The data are to be gathered within the established categories, so that for each category there is one or more standard and a factual description of the existing situation. These data may be gathered by testing, observing, interviewing, and other means.)
4. Compare the data with the standards. (In each category, take the data that describe the existing situation and appraise them in terms of the standard for that category. Note discrepancies, gaps, inadequacies, and the like.)
5. Interpret. (With the comparison before you, ask: What does this comparison say that is significant? What conclusions are justified? What lines of action are suggested?)

To illustrate the way in which these steps may be used, take the situation in which a person is attempting to evaluate himself as a student.

First, he decides on categories for analysis. He may decide on the following six categories:

His ability to read.
His ability to observe and listen.
His ability to detect ideas.
His ability to organize ideas.
His ability to weigh ideas.
His ability to use ideas.

Two tests ought to be applied to such a list of categories for analysis: (1) Does each category follow logically from those which precede it? (2) If each category were dealt with in the sequence suggested, would the total result be a truly comprehensive and adequate picture of the situation?

Second, he works out standards. In order to do this, he takes each of the categories and articulates one or more standards for each. For instance:

His ability to read. Suggested standard: Can cover, with good retention, twenty-five pages of serious religious material per hour.

His ability to observe and listen. Suggested standard: Produces meaningful and permanently useful notes.
His ability to detect ideas. Suggested standard: Grasps main points quickly, seeing relation of subordinate ideas and illustrations to the main points immediately.
Etc.

In each case the standard or standards represent specific instances of behavior appropriate to the category, providing norms against which actual behavior may be appraised.

Third, he gathers data. He times his reading. He reviews critically notes that he has taken. He keeps logs of his performance. He submits to review of his behavior and performance as a student by others. He undergoes periodic retesting.

Fourth, he compares the data with the standards. His performance (the data) in each category is reviewed in terms of the standards for the appropriately corresponding category.

Fifth, he interprets. Using this illustration of self-evaluation as a student, an excerpt from the interpretation might read:

This comparison locates my difficulty as that of inability to detect certain types of ideas. I am able to grasp concrete points when they are illustrated but am unable to grasp and illustrate for myself abstract and generalized statements. This is reflected, then, all along the line—in organizing, weighing, and using ideas. The place to begin corrective and remedial work is at the point of detection of ideas.

This illustration raises in a very direct way the question of the degree of specificity that ought to be achieved in objectives and standards. Is the appropriate objective for appraisal one of motivation or personal end, one of learning task, one of age-level attainment, one of anticipated behavioral outcome, or some other? The demand in education is usually for very specific objectives, so that in effect the objective becomes a standard or an anticipated behavioral outcome. This needs to be subjected to question.

Very specific standards work well in a situation such as that illustrated. This is where they are appropriate. Attempts have been made, as in *Junior High Objectives* (National Council of the Churches of Christ in the U.S.A., 1953), to be very specific about standards in every phase of the Christian education task. Valuable as such an attempt is, it also cannot fail to reveal its artificialities and inadequacies. For one thing, it can never be truly comprehensive; no list of standards will ever cover even the essentials in a specific way. Again, it tends to become legalistic; inevitably neglecting the spirit of the enterprise, it concentrates upon behaviors that may or may not represent its spirit adequately. Further, it becomes arbitrary, especially when it ties standards to age levels, as in *Junior High Objectives;* the twelve-year-old is described, the fourteen-year-old is described, and the curriculum stems from clues on how to influence growth from one level to the other. Lewis J. Sherrill, in his strictures against undue specificity in Christian education objectives, pointed out that by trying to be too definite in our standards we may actually be interfering with and hindering what is most important in Christian education.

The solution to this problem is to use specific standards but to subject them at all times to scrutiny in terms of the basic objective of Christian education. To subordinate them to the basic objective allows them to operate in evaluation in appropriate ways, but also guarantees that they will remain changeable. What is needed is the type of standard that is definite enough to be used in such a process as is illustrated above, but that is not permanently fixed nor considered to be applicable to every case.

The basic objective of Christian education is itself useful in evaluation, contrary to the belief of many Christian educators and evaluation specialists. In any Christian education situation, the questions may be asked: In what ways is the objective being achieved? To what degree is the objective being achieved? The answers to these questions are more than mere grist for the mill of evaluation; the very fact that there are positive answers to the questions in a given situation may very well be all that the Christian educator needs to know in order to be confident that Christian education is taking place. The unexpected, the unique, the unanticipated, is often more valuable than the expected, the usual, or the anticipated in Christian education.

When specific standards are used, how shall they be judged as to their validity? The tests of their validity might be: (1) Do they express, in some integral way, the intention of the objective of Christian education? (2) Are they clearly related to the scope of Christian education? (3) Do they obviously implement the process of Christian education? (4) Do they reflect the context of Christian education? In a negative way, a standard might be satisfactory if it did not run counter to any of these four essential ingredients of Christian education. But in a positive way, express connection between a standard and these basic ingredients tends to guarantee the standard's theological and pragmatic value.

Method in Individual Evaluation

Until there is some possibility of accurate appraisal using a less cumbersome method, the individual case study will remain the most reliable and valid method for personal evaluation in Christian education. The case study provides a rather comprehensive, and certainly holistic, approach to gathering data that may be used in the understanding of the individual's religious development. Even self-evaluation may be made an integral part of the case study method.

The case study is a method by which the person is looked at "whole" in a dynamic and realistic environment. In the case study, constellations of data are gathered concerning a person, providing a basis for interpretative appraisal of the person's attainment.

The problem of particular method is not hard to solve in the case study, since almost any variety of methods of gathering pertinent data may be used. To indicate the particular techniques that may be used, this sampling may be helpful:

Self-testing
Personal documents
Written and oral reports
Logs (diaries)
Projective techniques (simple ones such as finger painting may even be useful to amateur evaluators, while complex ones such as Rorschach testing are usable only by experts)
Interviewing (Allport has recently assured us that with normal persons—and most are normal —the same data will be gathered by simply asking persons about their motivations as by using the more devious projective techniques)
Observing
Anecdotal records (gathered by teachers, leaders, or observers)
Tests (tests of intelligence, ability and aptitude, achievement, interest, and personality)

With even a few of these techniques, significant insight into the person's situation and religious life may be gained.

The longitudinal problem presents itself, of course, as a complication in the case study. The case study can usually give a picture of the person only at one given time or in a limited time span. In order to increase the time span and to see the person in terms of developmental trends, data on the person's background and past history must be a part of the study. Even better is the keeping of good case study records for the person over a period of years, so that the case study and its insights may become cumulative. Unless this problem is solved, the judgments forthcoming from the case study can be only cross-sectional in character.

How are insights to be gained from, and judgments made on the basis of, the case study? Valid judgments from such data have been described as "clinical" in character. That is, with the data before him, the investigator considers the meaning they may hold first from this angle, then from that, until he has constructed an interpretation that appears to do real justice to the facts of the person's situation. This judgment is carefully submitted to the person himself, and to others who are authorized to participate in the evaluation and are capable of understanding the process of appraisal. In the long run, a working set of insights is forthcoming, upon which a future course of action for the person and those responsible for his education may proceed.

In order to be meaningful and useful, the case study must be based upon categories that are clearly comprehensive and analytical of the elements that are important in religious experience. To prevent slanting of interpretation, the categories should be those of religious experience but at the same time be capable of Christian interpretation if the data warrant such interpretation. In this light, the following categories are suggested for such case studies:

The person's activities. How he spends his time reveals to a great degree who he is. The investigator must be careful to include a typical day, the weekend, and the summer.

The person's enjoyments. Of his various activities, which does he select as those which give him pleasure? Which activities seem to him to be most rewarding? There is a rudimentary clue here to his value system, and thus to his real religion.

The person's loyalties. The investigator explores here the scope and depth of the person's definitive attachment to persons, institutions, and ideas. Where do Jesus Christ and the church figure in the person's loyalties? How do the strengths of his various loyalties compare with one another?

The person's alertness to value. How aware of meaning and value is this person? How alert is he to intellectual value—to truth? How alert is he to aesthetic value—to beauty? How alert is he to ethical value—to good? How alert is he to religious value—to the things of the spirit? What specific evidences are there of these kinds of awareness?

The person's faithfulness to value. How true is he to the meaning and value that he sees? How faithful is he to truth, to beauty, to good, and to the things of the spirit?

The level of the person's religious awareness. At one extreme of religious awareness one would simply know that there was such a thing as prayer and that others had experienced it. At the other extreme some would place the experience of mystical union. In between would be many other levels. At what level of religious awareness has this person arrived?

The cycles of the person's religious awareness. Religious awareness can never be sustained at a consistently high pitch. For some there is no cycle, however, since their religious awareness merely comes and goes without any predictable pattern. With others, however, there are definite periods of intensification of religious awareness on a daily cycle, on a weekly cycle, on a yearly cycle, or even on the basis of major events in the life span. (Daily devotions, the sabbath, and the seasons of the church year follow cycles.) To what cycle, if any, does this person's religious experience tend to correspond?

The cognitive and affective content of the person's participation in overtly religious activities. To put it simply: What is the person actually thinking and feeling as he attends church, studies the Bible, prays, or engages in any of the other activities that are considered to be religious?

As hinted at before, it may be useful to engage an "appraisal team" for interpreting (and for making) the case study. Such a team would consist of such persons as the individual himself, his teachers, leaders, parents, and any others who might at some particular point be able to contribute data or insights.

C. Ellis Nelson, of Union Theological Seminary in New York City, in discussing the matter of individual appraisal, has suggested that our preoccupation with development, behavior, process, movement, growth, and becoming in evaluation has perhaps obscured the category of being. The objective of Christian education can be a factor in correcting this situation, since it emphasizes the importance of "helping persons to *be* aware of God's self-disclosure and seeking love in Jesus Christ and to respond in faith and love." The longitudinal emphasis is essential, especially in differentiating the individual from the group stereotype; yet the emphasis on what he is and how he responds *now*, as distinct from what he has been or where he has come from, is equally important.

Nelson has also stressed the importance of considering the fact of the lateral expansion of the Christian life in evaluation, as well as the usual pyramidlike development. By this he means the deepening of the same kinds of experience, rather than the superimposition of new types of experience. Most of our attempts at evaluation have been rather exclusively oriented to the latter type of development.

Criteria for Individual Appraisal

Evidences of awareness and response are the data of individual appraisal. Through the use of such a method as the case study, the data may be gathered in terms of constellations of attitudes, skills, and concepts that characterize, and perhaps define, the individual at any given time. (By stressing "at any given time," the intention is not in any way to minimize the importance of the longitudinal. Rather, the longitudinal picture may be said to consist of a meaningful sequence of "given times.")

These constellations of evidences of awareness and response may be examined, using the objective of Christian education as the key to the criteria to be used. Standards of a "tentatively specific" kind may be well used at this point as the definite criteria for evaluation. But judgment, evaluation, and appraisal must proceed on the basis of both anticipated *and unanticipated* outcomes.

The key question to be raised in the appraisal at this point is, Do these constellations of evidences of awareness and response indicate consistency, meaningfulness, effectiveness, and appropriate response? The standards, tentatively specific as they are, will be suggestive of ways in which to answer this question. But the data themselves will suggest answers that have not been, and could not be, anticipated in any previously formulated standards.

The result of such an evaluation is a judgment of the degree to which the objective of Christian education has been attained in this person's life and experience, carefully differentiated from the life and experience of others in terms of his particular ways of being aware and responding, and indicating the nature of the process of religious living and development in his particular situation.

Records and Reports

As a matter of individual appraisal has been developed in this chapter, various suggestions have been made concerning the persons who may participate in the gathering of the data and in their interpretation. The importance of cumulative records, in order to provide the necessary sweep for longitudinal understanding, has been stressed.

The most important report on individual appraisal is to the person himself. To the degree that it rings true to him, he will take hold of its implications and act upon them. This is perhaps the most important reason why appraisal should not be considered a once-for-all matter. To come back periodically with new insights based upon new data, and to help the individual to see himself in this new light, has an obvious value far beyond a report given once and never supplemented.

Reports to others (teachers, leaders, parents) are called for to the extent that they are requested or needed, and also to the extent that they can be understood and used. Good reports given to persons unprepared to receive them are often misunderstood, resented, and misused. In any church or Christian education situation, appraisal must be accompanied by gradual training in the use of the results of appraisal, so that the individual and all persons concerned with him may make their plans for their future educational efforts on the basis of a realistic knowledge of the situation they deal with and of the persons involved.

2

APPRAISING PROGRAM AND PROCESS

THE APPRAISAL of program and process centers upon the evaluation of the institutions of Christian education and the way in which they are doing their work. The plan for evaluation that follows this chapter and occupies the rest of the book is an attempt to provide an approach to such appraisal. This chapter is intended to provide, in brief form, a rationale for the plan that is presented, to explain why the plan is as it is.

The institutions that seek to promote religious growth range, of course, from the home to ecumenical bodies. Yet the institution most often thought of in this connection is the local parish. Thus the plan that is suggested for Christian education evaluation concentrates on the work of the parish. This includes, however, not only the management aspects of the work of the parish, but even more important, the program and curriculum of Christian education, the dynamics of the teaching-learning process itself as it is used in the parish, and to a certain extent individual religious growth in the sense in which it was treated in Chapter I, "Appraising Individual Attainment." Policy, program, and product are all to be appraised in any really complete evaluation of Christian education work; all three are woven together in the plan that is proposed.

There is a theological dimension in institutional as well as individual appraisal. The theological dimension, even though it complicates evaluation and provides great theoretical difficulties for the scientific investigator, gives a depth and meaning to Christian education evaluation that would otherwise be lacking. In fact, without thorough attention to the theological dimension, Christian education evaluation would be so meaningless as to be impossible.

What is this theological dimension? Simply put, it is the assertion that in Christian education there is much more than meets the eye, and that this "more than meets the eye" consists of the dynamic work of God in man's midst: his purposes, his mighty acts, and the work of his Holy Spirit. The objective of Christian education is so put that it attempts to focus all of Christian education upon awareness of this "more than meets the eye" and upon response to it. Consistent attention and reference to the objective should enable the investigator to keep the theological dimension actively in focus.

Principles

Three basic principles are built into the suggested plan for evaluation of program and process in Christian education: (1) Evaluate "whole." (2) Evaluate on a long-term basis. (3) Evaluate co-operatively.

Evaluate "whole." Piecemeal evaluation does have its place. It is important for the individual teacher to weigh each particular session for himself and to plan for the future in terms of the insights that he gains into himself, the persons he is working with, and the methods being employed. When an emergency arises, as when attendance drops severely in a particular group, spot evaluation is called for.

Important as piecemeal evaluation can be, what is proposed here is that the entire program be looked at carefully and thoroughly. To that end, five areas have been defined that will cover the entire program and process in a manageable and understandable way:

Christian education in the congregation at large
Christian education in the family
The Christian education of children
The Christian education of youth
The Christian education of adults

Each of these areas is a clear and unmistakable center for Christian education in the parish; in each a number of different agencies of the parish and a number of types of activity in Christian education are gathered up; and attention to all five will guarantee that the investigation will cover the entire situation.

The committee on evaluation (which may very well be the same as the body in the local parish that is responsible for Christian education—the committee, board, commission, or council on Christian education), in order to handle its work comprehensively, needs five subcommittees or subgroups, each of which will concentrate on one of these five areas. Yet the committee itself needs to keep the groups working together, so that insights into the program may be shared and compared, to the end that the findings, recommendations, and resultant action may not be piecemeal.

Evaluate on a long-term basis. A useful evaluation cannot be done quickly. It takes time to prepare ourselves for evaluation; it takes time to gather data; it takes time to interpret data, to let insights come through and mature; it takes time to get reports ready, to get them read and digested, to get them discussed and analyzed; it takes time for people to make up their minds about the findings; it takes time to make, and accept, recommendations; it takes time to decide on practical and appropriate ways of carrying out recommendations; it takes time to effect the changes that are called for.

For the church that wants a quick taking of its pulse, there are many check lists available, particularly from denominational offices. These are useful, yet are necessarily superficial since they almost invariably involve the acceptance of objective and standards worked out by some body outside the parish. Even evaluation devices that help the parish to raise questions about purposes and standards often fail to estimate realistically the time and effort called for. The plan suggested in this book tries to go deep and also to be realistic about the time that must be taken. Evaluation like this is a long, hard process. But it is worth it, because it produces significant and lasting results.

Evaluate co-operatively. If the evaluation is to get the facts it needs, carry the parish along in the process, arrive at recommendations that will be accepted, and enlist the necessary persons in carrying out the recommendations, the basis of participation in the study at all points must be wide. This means co-operation at the proper points by pupils and other participants, by parents, by teach-ers and other leaders, by administrators, by the clergy, by other persons in the community (leaders of other community agencies, for instance), and by laymen.

The co-operative principle implies that evaluation of the Christian education program will probably take the form of self-study. Even though a "director" of the study can be very helpful, his role ought to be that of co-ordinator of a co-operative process rather than that of an expert who comes in to do a job for the church. The co-operative principle has implications for the make-up of the committees in the evaluation; they ought to consist of groups widely representative of the interests and activities to be studied. In accordance with the co-operative principle, a "workshop" atmosphere ought to prevail throughout the study, calling for thoughtful identification of the issues, mutual concern at the crucial points in the study, and real delving together into the problems and possibilities that are presented. In a project like this, unless a workshop atmosphere is maintained, there is likelihood that the results and recommendations may be disregarded or ignored by those most concerned with them. Co-operation also implies the careful use of the techniques of analysis and reconstruction of group processes in making the evaluation. Suggestions are appended to each step in the plan for looking back at the way in which the group carrying out the evaluation has been functioning in doing its work.

The Basic Steps

The basic steps in evaluation of program and process are fact-finding, the setting of standards, appraisal itself, and the making of decisions toward improvement. These four steps are built systematically into the suggested plan for institutional evaluation.

Fact-finding. The first step is to describe the existing situation. In order to arrive at such a description, every possible approach must be explored. Those persons are to be consulted who are most likely to have the desired information, and who can provide it fully, clearly, and accurately. In the suggested plan, the following approaches are used in gathering a full set of data on the situation in Christian education in the parish:

Basic historical, sociological, and operational data are gathered on the community and the parish.

Each group and its activities are canvassed.

Data on each teacher, leader, and administrator are secured.

Classes, groups, and committees are visited and observed in operation.

Participants are questioned about their activities and reactions.

Parents are asked to give their impressions and reactions.

Basic information is gathered on the church's work with and program for families.

Throughout the evaluation, the information collected in these ways is used by the appropriate subcommittees and by the evaluation committee itself. Vast amounts of material are involved; yet if care is exercised and sufficient time is taken to organize, digest, and mull over the information, the needed ideas and insights will emerge.

Setting standards. In order for evaluation to proceed, the facts must be examined in the light of appropriate standards. To set these standards in useful form means to proceed from the most basic principles of Christian education to a description of the particular ways in which these principles ought to apply in the parish that is being studied.

First, then, the basic principles (context, scope, purpose, process, and design) are to be established. These may be adopted from an authoritative source, or may be constructed on the spot. The advantage of the former way is that the basic principles are likely to be the product of the wisdom of a great many people, distilled from years of experience and thought. The advantage of the latter is that the basic principles will have direct local applicability and will have to be thought through by the parish with great care. The plan proposes that these two processes be combined, the strengths of both being used. Authoritative statements are suggested, but the particular parish is asked to react to them thoroughly and deeply enough to revise them completely, if need be.

With the basic principles of context, scope, purpose, process, and design established, the second step in setting standards is the detailed analysis of the task of Christian education in the parish. What are the particular functions to be performed and the essential operations to be taken care of? Many such operations and functions will be listed under such categories as:

Organization
Program
Curriculum
Personnel
Participation
Management
Building and equipment
Finance

The result of this analysis will be a comprehensive list of the functions, activities, and concerns of the Christian education program in the parish.

The third step is to provide specific standards (descriptions of the conditions that ought to obtain) for each of the items in the analysis just made. The suggested plan provides a sample list of such functions, activities, and concerns which the particular parish may adapt to its own purposes, and indicates how to proceed to construct the kind of detailed standards upon which the evaluation depends.

Appraisal itself. Once such specific standards are constructed, the comparison of the existing situation with the standards may proceed. For every function, activity, and concern in the analyzed list, the facts of the situation are to be compared with the standard or standards that are appropriate. The result will be a series of detailed judgments on points of adequacy and inadequacy, success and failure, fulfillment and need, in the program. The most significant findings are those in which needs are identified.

Decisions toward improvement. On the basis of the needs that have been identified, ideas and insights are required that will point the way toward improvement, toward the meeting of the needs. This, of course, is the point at which the evaluation takes on practical value in the parish.

If those who have been involved in the evaluation have gathered their facts carefully and thoroughly, if they have set their standards convincingly, and if they have produced a penetrating comparison of situation and standards, the stage is set for meaningful decisions toward improvement. Here again, however, the process cannot be hurried. Adequate time is needed to mull over the needs that have emerged, to see them from every possible angle, and to consider ways in which they might be met. Gradually, however, recommendations for improvement will begin to emerge.

To put these recommendations into practice requires that the process of co-operative self-study be consistently used from the beginning. If the persons responsible for carrying out the recommendations have been in on the study from the beginning, and either have played a role in formulating the recommendations or have been prepared to anticipate them, there is some possibility that faithful action may be taken in line with the recommendations that are made.

The Basic Methods

The methods that will best implement the principles and steps that have already been outlined are: the institutional case study, the workshop, reporting, and action research. All four are built into the proposed plan at the proper points.

The institutional case study. To make an institutional case study means to gather all the data necessary to get a profile of the parish, its community, and its work. Since one of the main phases of evaluation is the collecting of factual data for the purpose of describing the situation, the procedures involved in making an institutional case study seem especially appropriate.

Basic to the institutional case study is the process of social survey—the putting together of the information on the community and the parish that will enable the investigators to see the essential facts and trends in the situation. The method of social survey, however, needs to be supplemented in order that the dynamics—the flesh and blood—of the community and parish may become evident. Such supplementary materials may be secured and built into the basic material through such means as observation of various aspects of the program, the use of questionnaires to get additional facts and personal slants on the situation, opinion-taking (essentially a "live" use of the personal questionnaire), and interviewing (also a type of questionnaire, used to check and to supplement other data).

To take all the methods, to use them, and to secure from their use the information on the parish and community that will illuminate their conditions, is to make a start on an institutional case study. However, as with the individual case study, the investigators must mull over the data, seek to organize them meaningfully, and seek to let them tell what they have to say, before the "personality" or "character" of the parish and community can become clear. This further process of contemplating the data, meditating over them, and seeking to probe their meaning in depth is what makes the institutional case study different from the more limited "survey." For purposes of understanding a

Christian education program well enough to be able to evaluate it, the added dimension of the case study is required.

The workshop. As the term is now used in educational circles, a "workshop" is a gathering, usually several days or weeks in length, in which persons concerned with a particular problem or group of problems come together to clarify their difficulties, to identify the resources that are available for dealing with them, to get expert help in the process, and to construct solutions and action programs that seem to hold promise. In religious circles, meetings like "conferences," "consultations," and "retreats" often include elements to be found in educational workshops.

The workshop experience is particularly useful in Christian education evaluation at several crucial points. When objectives and basic principles are to be identified, discussed, and decided on, the workshop atmosphere is exactly the climate in which lasting results may be forthcoming. When needs are to be identified in appraisal, the workshop situation will include the people who need to be involved and who will be in a position to say what the data mean so far as strengths and weaknesses, successes and failures, adequacies and inadequacies, and fulfillments and needs are concerned. In deciding on recommendations, the workshop is again the proper setting, since the people who must take the recommendations and carry through on them can be considering the data, standards, and needs, and their implications, side by side with others who have had other responsibilities in the evaluation.

Thus, in the plan that is proposed in this book, the workshop plan is used at five strategic points:

Setting basic principles
Interpreting these principles for each of the five areas of concern
Setting standards
Appraisal, and identification of needs
Decision toward improvement

The workshop technique has been used in similar fashion by the Protestant Episcopal Church in its parish-life conferences, and in more modified form by many local parishes in their planning retreats.

Reporting. When data have been gathered and organized, it is important to get them before the people who are interested and concerned. The first written report proposed for the evaluation is thus the report on the facts. A good report should be self-interpreting as it is read. Self-interpretation may be facilitated by simple, graphic presentation of the main findings, and by careful attention to the logic and interest of the report. But reporting on the facts may go beyond the preparation and dissemination of a written report; exhibits, displays, bulletins, and meetings for explaining the report can help to create interest and to spread the information that is gathered, so that it may be known and considered by as wide a circle as possible.

The second report proposed deals with our objectives. Here again the widest circulation and fullest consideration are desirable. In order to secure such circulation and consideration, methods like those suggested for the report on the facts may be used.

The third and fourth reports are those on appraisal, and plans for the future. By the time these reports are made and considered, a great deal of spadework toward understanding and using them will have been done through the use of the first two reports. Each report builds on the preceding ones, both as to content and as to use.

The standard procedure for reporting, then, should be the formulation, issuing and use of one report at a time, until all four are available. The steps in the case of each report are these:

Formulation of the report
Distribution of the report
Study and interpretation of the report
Building opinion toward action on the basis of the report

Clearly, reporting is not a matter of attaching "Finis" to a particular part of the evaluation; rather, reporting is the way in which findings, suggestions, and recommendations are transferred from those persons who have been closest to the evaluation to those who are widely responsible for the program. Reporting may be interpreted as an essential step between study and action.

Action research. The kind of evaluation that is proposed in this book is so comprehensive and far-reaching that there should be no need to repeat it except at fairly long intervals. It should, however, stimulate leaders and groups in the church to do evaluation and research on their own work and programs as follow-up for the more thorough evaluation. As a matter of fact, this kind of ongoing study is the most appropriate kind of result of the establishment of a sense of need for evaluation in the parish.

Action research provides a suitable framework for this continuing study of program and process. It is a problem-identifying and problem-solving procedure that may be used by a teacher and his class, a leader and his group, or a committee at any time, accompanying and enriching their regular work. Although there may very well be considerable co-ordination of effort in action research in a parish, the initiative for it rests primarily with the individual leader or group.

The steps in action research, as developed in the proposed plan, are these:

Identification of a problem
Formulation of possible solutions
Gathering of data to test the possible solutions
Selection of the most promising solution
Trying out the solution chosen
Evaluation of the solution
Identification of emergent new problems

With an active and shared program of this kind, applied to a variety of problems of group life and parish activity, the effects of the evaluation may be not only kept alive but considerably enhanced as time goes on. When the time comes to restudy the parish's Christian education program thoroughly again, those persons who are trained in evaluation through action research will be in a position to be particularly helpful in pursuing the evaluation skillfully and meaningfully.

Dangers

As a warning of some of the more common pitfalls that may cause trouble in evaluation, certain dangers may be enumerated. Alert to these, the committees doing the evaluation, and the parish at large, may successfully avoid them.

Premature evaluation is to be avoided. There must be time for planting and for growth before appraisal. If evaluation is undertaken too soon, it may actually interfere with growth and maturation toward the ends of Christian education.

Constant evaluation is to be avoided. If the mood of evaluation becomes a constant in Christian education in the parish, the stability of the program is likely to be threatened. Periodic evaluation, timed judiciously to take advantage of points where real questions and dilemmas have arisen or where advances are possible, is far more useful than constant evaluation.

Nervous evaluation is to be avoided. Some persons and groups feel that evaluation must be undertaken, especially when they are unsure of, or confused about, their program of Christian education. Such evaluation too often grows out of personal or group insecurity, and takes the form of rationalization and excuse-making. Nervous evaluation defeats the purposes of genuine evaluation, and can give the whole process such a bad reputation as to make genuine evaluation impossible in a given parish.

√ Compulsive evaluation is to be avoided. Compulsive evaluation is evaluation for its own sake, rather than for the sake of the effectiveness of program and process. There are persons who "can't wait to get to that part of the meeting"! There are persons who complain when a meeting is properly over, "But we haven't evaluated it!"

√ Cutting the program to fit the demands of evaluation is to be avoided. In some Christian education circles there is a peculiar logic that holds: (1) All program, process, and product is to be evaluated. (2) There are many elements that may go into program and process that cannot be evaluated or that would be exceedingly difficult to evaluate. (3) Therefore, leave these out, and include in the curriculum only elements that can be evaluated. Such logic, when exposed in this fashion, is obviously faulty; yet infatuation with particular means of evaluation can lead persons to feel that nothing worthy can be produced by methods or materials that do not lend themselves to their particular evaluative devices. The basic principle that is violated in such cases is that curriculum decisions are always inadequate if they are made in the light of administrative considerations. Just as the curriculum must serve the objective, so administration (including evaluation) must serve the curriculum.

√ Uncritical use of nontheological educational assumptions is to be avoided. The easiest kinds of learning to evaluate are those that result from educational methods based upon behavioristic assumptions about man. The methods of evaluation involved are neat, and the findings are usually fairly clear-cut. Neat as these methods of evaluation are, they are not to be used uncritically in Christian education, since the assumptions about man upon which they are based are quite alien to a Christian theological understanding of man. Educational assumptions, and theories and methods of evaluation built upon them, need to be in harmony with the insights of Christian theology in order to be useful in Christian education. If the sug-

gestions made in this book seem cumbersome, one of the reasons is that decisions have had to be made about evaluation and its methods that were not always the most simple and direct, the theological understanding of man and the church being considered to be primary.

Summary

The position and plan of evaluation proposed in this book may be summarized in four statements. These deal with *institutional self-study, study of program and curriculum, evaluating the teaching-learning process,* and *remaining "in character" in evaluation.*

In *evaluating the institutions* that seek to promote religious growth, it is useful to undertake surveys and institutional case studies. Information is to be sought on:

Purposes
Setting
Relationships: internal, and to the community and other institutions
Organization
Program
Personnel and leadership
Participation and membership
Management
Building and equipment
Finance
Etc.

Evaluation is often in the form of institutional self-study by a regularly constituted committee or by one especially appointed for this purpose, but it may also be conducted with expert help from outside (denominational field people, university research groups, or other similar "experts").

In *evaluating program and curriculum*, it is well to undertake both survey and theoretical analysis, which involves periodic scrutiny of basic purposes, the interests and needs of participants, standards, and available resources. This may be done at any level of program and curriculum, for a total parish, for a denomination, or for any other agency or group that has responsibility for Christian education.

In *evaluating the teaching-learning process itself,* it is well to use "live" supervision; teacher-observer teams; group self-supervision; group process techniques; and particularly such forms of self-study and decision as the workshop, conference, consultation, or retreat.

In evaluating, *a church must remain "in character."* That is, the church must *be* the church as it evaluates. The methods it uses must be characteristic of the church—the community of faith—in action. In fact, the evaluation should be such that the church will gain deep insight into what it means to be the church. This may be accomplished in part by being sure that the evaluation expresses the heart of the church's life and purpose in the nature of the objective that is adopted and used. In part, it may be accomplished by being sure that the way of conducting the evaluation includes at its heart the church's way of living its life and doing its work: worship, prayer, and live expectation of the work of the Holy Spirit in its midst. It may also be accomplished by enduring concern for change—change toward adequacy in institutional organization, program, management, and supervision.

Part Two
A PLAN FOR LOCAL PARISH APPRAISAL IN CHRISTIAN EDUCATION

3

EVALUATING YOUR CHRISTIAN EDUCATION PROGRAM

PERIODIC evaluation is required if the church is to do a significant and creative job in Christian education. There are four aspects of the work that need to be evaluated: individual religious growth, the teaching-learning process, program and curriculum materials, and the way the congregation and the home are doing their work. Without ignoring the first three, this guide centers its attention upon the effectiveness of Christian education in the congregation and the home. A plan is offered for the study and evaluation of the whole educational work of the church in its parish.

What Does It Mean to Evaluate?

The evaluation of the Christian education program of the church is a matter of fact-finding and appraisal, in order that a sound foundation may be laid for next steps. Fact-finding provides the sober, comprehensive picture of the existing situation. Appraisal shows the existing situation in comparison with what it should be.

Evaluation through fact-finding and appraisal may be accomplished by any church that wishes to examine its Christian education program, if it will try to answer these five questions about its work:

1. *What are the facts about our situation?* The church surveys itself in order to get a factual description of its program and work.

2. *What are our objectives?*

3. *What are we accomplishing?* At this point the church appraises itself, comparing the facts about its situation with its objectives, carefully noting specific strengths and weaknesses.

4. *What, then, do we need?* Taking account of the strengths and weaknesses that have been shown to exist in its Christian education program, and looking at them in the light of its objectives, the points at which improvement is needed are identified and listed.

5. *What next steps shall we take?* The church then studies the ways in which the needed improvements might be made, weighs the various possibilities, decides on courses of action that give promise of accomplishing the desired ends, and assigns responsibility for getting the work done.

Who Shall Conduct the Evaluation?

Effective evaluation takes place when it is guided and co-ordinated by the individuals and groups who have major responsibility for the Christian education program, and when it involves in addition active participation by all those who have a stake in it—teachers, leaders, pupils, groups, officers, professional workers, church members, community leaders, neighbors, and others.

Evaluation is going on all the time, whether it is guided and co-ordinated or not. The individual participant evaluates what is going on, what is happening to him, and his response in terms of the meaning and relevance (or lack of meaning and relevance) to him. The group evaluates in terms of the worth (or lack of worth) of the goals toward which it is striving, and its achievement (or failure to reach achievement) of those goals. The person who guides a group—leader, teacher, officer, or professional worker—is forced by circumstances to evaluate the plans, process, and results of the enterprises for which he has responsibility. The congregation evaluates as it asks in various ways, What is the task of the community of faith in this place at this time? The church's neighbors evaluate as they estimate its worth and pass judgment on its effectiveness.

The element that may be lacking is the "over-all look" at the program, a plan that will:

—bring to light the evaluation that is going on;
—shed light on other aspects of the program that need investigation and appraisal;
—guide and co-ordinate the evaluative process systematically.

The proposal here is that the committee, commission, or council responsible for Christian education in the local church take the initiative in guiding and co-ordinating the study of the program, and that this committee seek the active co-operation of others in the church and community at every point. In this way the church may be sure that there will be no "final report" to be turned over for action to persons who have been made skeptical and resentful because they have been left out along the way. Rather, the whole church will be learning how to evaluate and set in motion a continuing process of co-operative evaluation that can serve its changing needs.

The committee, commission, or council on Christian education in the local congregation is usually made up of those persons best qualified to think through the congregation's Christian education problems, determine policy, and work out the general lines of program. This group is directly responsible to the governing bodies of the church, usually deriving its authority from and reporting to those bodies; its membership also is likely to overlap considerably with that of the governing bodies of the congregation. It is also in close touch with, or has among its members, those who are responsible for the major aspects of the program, that is, those persons who have responsibility for the church school, youth work, adult program, and other aspects of Christian education in the parish. More than any other group related to the Christian education program, this committee, commission, or council is in a position to be objective in its judgments and recommendations, since its membership and tasks make it likely to be less emotionally involved in any one part of the existing program than other groups might be. By virtue of its tasks, its contacts, and its approach, therefore, this is the group in the church best equipped to act as the committee on evaluation of the Christian education program.

In order to guide and co-ordinate the total study, the committee must give attention to those activities of the congregation at large that are educational in nature, the activities of the families of the church as they engage in Christian education, and the Christian education of children, youth, and adults. In a very small church the committee should designate one person for each of these areas, to pull information together and to guide evaluation. In other churches there should be subcommittees to guide fact-finding, appraisal, and decision on next steps in each area. The setup for evaluation would be as follows:

The areas of concern of the subcommittees on family life, children's work, youth work, and adult work are obvious. The concerns of the subcommittee on Christian education in the congregation at large may not be so clear. What is meant by "Christian education in the congregation at large" is the teaching effect of all the congregation does—the way it is set up to do its work, the way it worships, the way it expresses its concern for the community and the world, the way it undertakes its evangelistic work, the way its boards reach decisions, and the way financial matters are handled, for instance. These may not seem to be exactly "educational" in nature, yet they do educate. The reasons why these matters should be handled by a separate subcommittee are that the groups involved are usually representative of more than one age level, and that unless these matters are lifted up for special attention, they are likely to be overlooked as part of the educational work of the congregation.

COMMITTEE ON EVALUATION (in most cases the same as the committee, commission, or council responsible for Christian education)				
Working with appropriate participants, leaders, and neighbors				
Through subcommittees, guiding evaluation of				
Christian education in the congregation at large	Christian education in families	Children's work	Youth work	Adult work

The evaluation will be most effectively accomplished if one person is given responsibility for guiding it—the minister, the director of Christian education, a representative of the denomination, or an especially capable lay leader. This will assure co-ordination, since this person can keep the over-all plan in mind, and help the committee, subcommittees, and others to answer the basic questions and prepare the necessary reports. This person may also help those involved to deepen their theological understanding of the church and its educational functions, and to deepen their understanding of the values in the processes of evaluation.

What is proposed is a process of co-operative evaluation. Therefore, in addition to the committee and its subcommittees (or responsible individuals), the following have important roles to play in the evaluation:

—The officers and leaders of the various Christian education groups in the church.

Role: To provide information about their groups and to consult with the committee in arriving at findings and conclusions about the program as a whole.

—Teachers, group leaders, and others with responsibility for group leadership and administration.

Role: To give information on their work, and to help the committee (and especially its subcommittees) to arrive at decisions on improvement with regard to the aspects of the program with which they have to do.

—Observers.

Role: Especially appointed to visit the various groups, watch them in action, interpret their work, and analyze their needs and potential.

—Participants in the program (pupils, members, etc.).

Role: To provide information concerning their participation and what it means to them, and to help in reaching practical and relevant conclusions.

—Parents.

Role: To give information about their participation in, reactions to, and suggestions for, the program.

—Other members of the congregation.

Role: To provide information, and to participate in consultations on objectives, evaluation, and planning.

—Neighbors (responsible and informed persons from the community).

Role: To provide information, and to participate in consultations on objectives, evaluation, and planning.

How Shall the Evaluation Be Conducted?

In order to evaluate the church's program of Christian education, the committee constructs, considers, and builds upon an *institutional case study.* This institutional case study consists of a complete factual description of the significant aspects of the program. Thus a "profile" of the local Christian education work is provided. The case study also includes the data and suggestions that are required to appraise and redesign the program.

To construct an institutional case study of the Christian education program of the church, and to use it to the full, involves the co-operative use of three processes: *surveying, consulting, and reporting.* Surveying establishes the facts of the situation. Consulting provides the setting in which objectives may be determined, the facts of the survey interpreted, and the implications for action brought out. Reporting summarizes the findings, suggests conclusions, and lays the matter before all concerned.

When a survey of a local church's program of Christian education is undertaken, the objectivity of the approach is important: What are the unvarnished facts about the situation? A complete evaluation, while one of its aims is this complete factual description of the program, is concerned with at least two other matters: first, the goals the program is set up to achieve, and second, the actual carrying out of next steps toward reaching them. In order that goals may be defined and appropriate next steps be taken, the evaluation scheme itself must be set up so that its very procedures are educational, that is, likely to produce changing attitudes and methods on the part of those responsible for the program. This is why consultation and reporting are used in addition to surveying, and why all three processes are to be carried out in thoroughly co-operative ways.

Seeking co-operation of all involved in the program to survey, consult, and report may slow things down somewhat, since give-and-take is needed in planning for evaluation, gathering information, weighing findings, and drawing conclusions. It may also slow things down because differences may develop and have to be resolved. Evaluation, however, is useless unless its aims, procedures, findings, and conclusions are accepted by those involved in the program—and co-operation, even if it does slow things down, is the key to acceptance and to the resolution of conflict.

One is willing to have his work evaluated if he may have a hand in planning the evaluation, conducting it, drawing conclusions, and helping to decide on how next steps will be put into effect. The participants—groups and individuals—are interested in evaluation under the same conditions. In such a climate, the Christian educator is willing that differences should develop, since there is real promise of their creative resolution.

The committee's role (and that of the subcommittees charged with specific responsibilities) is therefore that of guiding and co-ordinating an evaluation process in which all concerned participate at every important point. "Group processes," techniques by which participation in co-operative fact-finding and decision-making is made possible, are the very heart of the matter.

As the committee follows the steps suggested in the construction and use of the institutional case study, the detailed ways in which participants and leaders may become involved are suggested in the sections on procedure. Suggestions are also made on how the committee may reflect from time to time on the effectiveness of its own procedures in carrying out the study. Appropriate forms are provided following the analysis of the steps in the evaluation.

The time required for this evaluation will vary considerably from church to church. Among the churches that participated in the field testing of the plan, several found it possible to complete the evaluation in four to six weeks. Others, however, estimated that it would take them from six months to a year to finish the study and to get the information and guidance from it that they wanted. The plan may, of course, be modified so as to cut down the time required. Details of such modification are best worked out by the individual church itself. One church suggested a lengthy period of preparation for the study: "Before an evaluation is started there should be at least a six-month introduction and acquaintance period. During this time all the Christian education groups in the church should become intimately acquainted with the objectives, mechanics, and over-all plan. Only when all concerned are very familiar with these matters should the actual fact-gathering begin."

4

THE PLAN IN BRIEF

THE PLAN for evaluation calls for a committee on evaluation, working through five subcommittees, asking five basic questions, and making four reports. The plan may be outlined as follows:

The Committee on Evaluation (preferably the same as the local congregation's committee, commission, or council on Christian education):

Works through five subcommittees, dealing with:
1. Christian education in the congregation at large
2. Christian education in the family
3. The Christian education of children
4. The Christian education of youth
5. The Christian education of adults

Asks five basic questions:
1. What are the facts about our situation?
2. What are our objectives?
3. What are we accomplishing?
4. What, then, do we need?
5. What next steps shall we take?

Makes four reports:
1. *Facts on Christian Education in Our Church*
2. *Our Objectives in Christian Education*
3. *An Appraisal of Christian Education in Our Church*
4. *A Plan of Action for Christian Education in Our Church*

5

PRELIMINARY PLANNING

THE EVALUATION begins by laying the foundations for information-gathering and analysis, focusing the talents and knowledge of a great many people in the church and community.

Procedures

The preliminary planning for the evaluation may be accomplished by the Committee on Evaluation, working as a whole, taking the following seven steps. When these steps have been taken, the structure will be complete for the evaluation, and the place and use of Forms A through G will be clear.

Four meetings of the Committee on Evaluation are recommended for this preliminary planning:

> First meeting: Steps 1-3, below
> Second meeting: Step 4, below
> Third meeting: Step 5, below
> Fourth meeting: Step 6, below

If the committee wishes to do the job of preliminary planning in a shorter period, the following plan for two meetings might be tried:

> First meeting: Steps 1-4, below
> Second meeting: Steps 5-6, below

1. Organize the committee:
   a. The committee needs a chairman, vice-chairman, and secretary. These officers may act as the group responsible for co-ordination of reports and for editorial work on the study.
   b. Subcommittees are to be appointed to guide and co-ordinate the study and evaluation of Christian education in:
      The congregation at large
      Family life
      Children's work
      Youth work
      Adult work
   c. Decide what the following are to be asked to do: groups, leaders, observers, partici-

pants, parents, other members of the church, and neighbors.
2. Review the guide, deciding on a plan that utilizes the guide's basic ideas and that is practicable in the local situation.
3. Formulate in a general way, for the committee's use and for use in meetings and consultations with others involved in the study:
   a. A statement of the reasons for evaluating the program.
   b. A statement of what you hope the evaluation will accomplish.
   c. A statement of the way in which you plan to conduct the study. (For instance, the study is to be conducted in a thoroughly co-operative way with all involved; it will interpret and evaluate on the basis of facts as they are discovered; it will be conducted as a self-study; etc.)
4. Prepare the following lists:
   a. A list of all the groups that are part of the church's program of Christian education, together with a list of those who would be designated as "officers and leaders of the various Christian education groups of the church." (These are the groups and persons involved with the analysis of groups and their activities, Form B.) For instance:
      The governing body
      The committee on Christian education
      Finance committees
      Other committees and councils
      Divisions and departments of the Sunday church school
      Vacation church school
      Weekday church school
      Special classes (parents, adults, communicants, etc.)
      The various groups in the youth fellowship
      Other age-level or special-interest groups

(young adults, college students, older
adults, etc.)

Clubs
Scouts
Choirs
Women's groups
Men's groups
Classes and groups for leadership education
Neighborhood groups
Small study, prayer, and discussion groups
Parents' groups
Sunday evening fellowship, and its groups
Home and extension service
Camps
Weekday nursery school

b. A list of all the officers, leaders, teachers, and others with responsible positions in the church's program of Christian education. (These are the teachers, leaders, and administrators who fill out Form C.) For instance:

Minister
Director of Christian education
Church school superintendents (general, divisional, departmental, vacation, weekday, etc.)
Other officers of the church school
Teachers
Group leaders
Members of the committee on Christian education (including members of its subcommittees)
Youth officers and advisers
Officers of men's and women's groups
Choir directors
Custodians

5. Assign to a temporary committee the responsibility for preparing the forms for the study. This committee will:

a. Go over all the forms carefully and will recommend:

The forms to be used in your particular church
Additional questions that need to be asked
Questions that should be deleted
Questions whose wording should be altered

b. See that the forms that are needed are reproduced in sufficient quantity for the study.

6. Plan for the following consultations (in this order):

a. A consultation with informed and responsible persons in the congregation (including leaders not identified specifically with Christian education) and the community (school people, community service people, persons with civic responsibilities, persons from other churches—councils of churches, youth councils, etc.).

b. A consultation with the officers and leaders of the various Christian education groups in the church.

c. Consultations of subcommittees with teachers, group leaders, and others with responsibility for group leadership and administration.

d. A consultation of the subcommittee on family life with representative members of the congregation.

e. Consultations of observers with age-level subcommittees and representatives of the groups to be visited.

7. Analyze and evaluate the procedures used in preliminary planning.

What evidence is there that roles (guiding, co-ordinating, information-giving, etc.) have been clarified, accepted, and used?

What roles have developed that were not anticipated?

In what ways may they be used to further the aims of the study? In what ways must they be transformed in order that the study may achieve its aims?

What evidence is there that a sense of comradely participation is developing in connection with the study? How widespread is it?

What evidence is there that a sense of co-operative search for facts and new ideas is beginning to develop? How widespread is it?

In what ways might the committee and its subcommittees remake their plans and procedures to make the study more widely accepted and useful?

How do individual members of the committees, and others participating, see and evaluate their roles?

How do individual members of the committees, and others participating, see and evaluate the work of the study as a whole?

6

ANSWERING THE QUESTION, "WHAT ARE THE FACTS ABOUT OUR SITUATION?" AND PREPARING THE REPORT *FACTS ON CHRISTIAN EDUCATION IN OUR CHURCH*

MEANINGFUL evaluation requires possession of the facts about the program that is being studied. At this point the committee and its subcommittees go to work, and enlist many others also, to get the facts about the Christian education program of the church.

What do the facts, once gathered, say? In order to realize their total impact without sacrificing detail, the study undertakes to analyze them and to set them forth in a report, *Facts on Christian Education in Our Church*. In this form they will be readily usable when they are to be interpreted later, and when they are to be evaluated by comparing them with the objectives.

Procedures

First, hold the following consultations, which have been prepared for:

1. The consultation of the Committee on Evaluation with members of the congregation and with informed and responsible persons from the community.
   a. Use the following agenda:
      Explain the evaluation.
      Enlist co-operation.
      Gather certain basic information (Form A).
      Make arrangements for continued assistance in formulating objectives, in appraising, and in drawing conclusions from the study.
   b. Prepare Form A.
   c. Turn over appropriate sections of Form A to the subcommittee on Christian education in the congregation at large.
2. The consultation of the Committee on Evalua-

tion with officers and leaders of the various Christian education groups in the church.
   a. Use the following agenda:
      Explain the evaluation.
      Enlist co-operation.
      Arrange for having Form B ("Analysis of a Group and Its Activities") filled out.
      Arrange for having the teachers, leaders, and others with responsibility for group leadership fill out Form C.
      Explain the role of the observers in the study (see Form D).
      Explain the role of program participants in the study (see Form E).
      Explain the role of parents in the study (see Form F).
      Explain the study of Christian education in the families of the parish (see Form G).
      Explain the role of the other members of the congregation in the study.
      Explain the role of the church's neighbors in the study.
      Receive questions and suggestions on the study.
   b. Receive, study, and prepare a general report on Forms B and C.
   c. Turn over appropriate findings to the subcommittees on children's work, youth work, and adult work.
3. Consultations of the subcommittees on children's work, youth work, and adult work with teachers, group leaders, and others who have responsibility for group leadership and for administration.
   a. Use the following agenda:
      Explain the evaluation.

Enlist co-operation.

Select the observers, clarify their role, and arrange for their visits to the various groups.

Select participants from various groups to be asked to fill out Form E, and make arrangements for having them do so.

Select parents to be asked to fill out Form F, and make arrangements for having them do so.

b. Receive, study, and report on Forms E and F, and appropriate sections of Forms B and C.

c. Share the information from Form F with the subcommittee on family life.

d. Prepare preliminary reports on:
"Facts on Our Children's Work"
"Facts on Our Youth Work"
"Facts on Our Adult Work"
Confine these reports strictly to factual data.
Submit them to the Committee on Evaluation.

4. The consultation of the subcommittee on family life with representatives of the congregation.
a. Use the following agenda:
Investigate the family life situation in the congregation.
Make plans for the use of Form G ("Christian Education in the Family").
Study the results of the use of Form F ("Parents' Questionnaire") by the age-level subcommittees.

b. Receive, study, and report on Form G.

c. Study findings of Form F and correlate these with the subcommittee's other findings.

d. Prepare a preliminary report on: "Facts on Christian Education in the Families of Our Church."
Confine this report strictly to factual data.
Submit it to the Committee on Evaluation.

5. Consultations of subcommittees on children's work, youth work, and adult work with observers, including representatives of the groups to be visited.
a. Use the following agenda:
Explain the purpose of the observation visits.
Decide on procedures and arrangements for the visits.
Explain the use of Form D ("Observation of a Group").

Train the observers through the role-playing of observation visits.
Study, analyze, and interpret the observations that are made.

b. Correlate the findings of the observations with the reports of the age-level subcommittees.

At the same time that these consultations are being held, the subcommittee on Christian education in the congregation at large should meet to:

a. Go over Form A and the reports from the consultations of the Committee on Evaluation and the subcommittee on Christian education in the family, to discover what is being done by the congregation at large in the way of Christian education.

b. Prepare a preliminary report on: "Facts on Christian Education in the Congregation at Large."
Confine this report strictly to the factual data.
Submit it to the Committee on Evaluation.

After the consultations and meetings are held, Forms A through G prepared, and preliminary reports submitted by the subcommittees, the Committee on Evaluation prepares the report *Facts on Christian Education in Our Church*, using the following outline:

FACTS ON CHRISTIAN EDUCATION IN OUR CHURCH

I. BASIC INFORMATION

A. What do the facts say about our history?
Source: Form A, section II.

B. What do the facts say about our church's community?
Sources: Form A, sections III and IX.
Form G, sections I and VI.

C. What do the facts say about our membership?
Sources: Form A, section IV.
Form B, section II.
Form C, questions 14, 15, and 24.
Form D, section IV.
Form E.
Form F, section I.
Form G, section I.

D. What do the facts say about our purposes?
Sources: Form B, questions 3 and 26.
Form C, questions 11, 26, and 32.
Form D, questions 1 and 2.
Form E.
Form F, questions 13, 14, and 15.

39

E. What do the facts say about our curriculum?
Sources: Form A, sections VI, VIII, and XV.
Form B, sections IV, V, and VI.
Form C, questions 12, 16-20.
Form D, sections II and III.
Form E.
Form F, questions 11, 12, 14, 18, and 20.
Form G, sections II-VI.

F. What do the facts say about our administration (including organization, management, and supervision)?
Sources: Form A, sections V, VII, IX-XIV, and XVI.
Form B, sections III, VII, VIII, and X.
Form C, section I and questions 13, 21-23, 25, 27, 29-31, 33, and 34.
Form D, sections IV and V.
Form F, questions 9-12 and 17-19.
Form G, sections II and V.

G. What do the facts say about our problems?
Sources: Form B, question 28.
Form C, question 28.
Form D, question 29.
Form F, question 16.
(As they are appropriate and useful, include spot maps. Secure a reasonably large map of the area. Spot the membership on it, using different-colored pencils to indicate residences of members in different classifications. Include graphs and charts showing membership trends, financial trends, etc.)

II. FACTS ON CHRISTIAN EDUCATION IN THE CONGREGATION AT LARGE
Source: Preliminary report from the subcommittee on the congregation at large.

III. FACTS ON CHRISTIAN EDUCATION IN THE FAMILIES OF OUR CHURCH
Source: Preliminary report from the subcommittee on family life.

IV. FACTS ON OUR CHILDREN'S WORK
Source: Preliminary report from the subcommittee on children's work.

V. FACTS ON OUR YOUTH WORK
Source: Preliminary report from the subcommittee on youth work.

VI. FACTS ON OUR ADULT WORK
Source: Preliminary report from the subcommittee on adult work.

VII. IMPLICATIONS
The Committee on Evaluation prepares this section on implications after the rest of the report is complete. This section should deal with such questions as these:
What trends are indicated by the facts?
What problems are brought out by the facts?
What questions are raised by the facts?

Have the report duplicated and ready for distribution in connection with answering the question, "What are we accomplishing?" and the preparation of the report *An Appraisal of Christian Education in Our Church.*

Analyze and evaluate the procedures used through this section of the study:

What indications are there that the procedures of the study are increasingly clear to all concerned? That they are not clear?

What indications are there that the subcommittees are clear on their tasks and relationships? That they are not clear?

As individuals and groups have expressed apprehensions they may have about the study or about their work in relation to the study, what has been done to reinterpret the study to them and to take their misgivings and suggestions seriously?

In what ways have the consultations proven to be effectively conducted? ineffectively conducted? What changes would be desirable in consultation procedures, looking forward to the involvement of these same people in appraisal of the program and plans for the future?

What leadership and membership roles have been assumed by participants in the process?

How may group productivity be increased and participation enhanced in the steps still ahead?

In what ways have the participants shown evidences of growth since the beginning of the study?

What indications are there that the report *Facts on Christian Education in Our Church* is accepted as a truly factual report on which the evaluation study can proceed to work toward interpretation, appraisal, and future planning?

7

ANSWERING THE QUESTION, "WHAT ARE OUR OBJECTIVES?" AND PREPARING THE REPORT *OUR OBJECTIVES IN CHRISTIAN EDUCATION*

A GOOD PROGRAM of Christian education is built to be an effective instrument in achieving the objective of Christian education in the life of the individual, the family, and the parish. Such a program involves the whole field of relationships, and focuses on helping persons "to be aware of God's self-disclosure and seeking love in Jesus Christ and to respond in faith and love, to the end that they may know who they are and what their human situation means, grow as sons of God rooted in the Christian community, live in the Spirit of God in every relationship, fulfill their common discipleship in the world, and abide in the Christian hope." (From *The Objective of Christian Education for Senior High Young People.*)

Evaluation always implies the comparison of a situation with the appropriate objectives that the situation is supposed to employ and embody. The study now centers on a fundamental understanding of objectives and their implications for the Christian education program of the local church.

Procedures

Make the following materials available to the members of the Committee on Evaluation and to the members of the subcommittees, and ask them to become thoroughly familiar with them.

The Objectives of Christian Education. National Council of Churches, 1958.

The Objective of Christian Education for Senior High Young People. National Council of Churches, 1958.

Your denomination's statement of the objectives of Christian education.

Have a meeting of the Committee on Evaluation, at which Form H is studied and completed. This will result in a general statement of objectives for Christian education in your church, covering these five key issues:

The church's task
The scope of Christian education
The purpose of Christian education
The process of Christian education
The way Christian education, as a program, is to be set up

Although more than one meeting may be needed to complete this statement, especially if there are any marked differences of point of view that need to be discussed, it should be possible to do the work fairly quickly if copies of Form H are given to the committee members well ahead of time, with the request that they study it carefully and write out drafts of their own views on the five key issues.

Give the complete statement of objectives to each of the subcommittees. Ask them to have meetings in which they study all five sections of the statement and put down in writing what they see as the implications of these objectives (the church's task, the scope of Christian education, the purpose of Christian education, the process of Christian education, and the setup for Christian education) for:

The congregation at large
The family
Children's work
Youth work
Adult work

To illustrate, the subcommittee on youth work, studying the general statement of objectives, is asked to report on these five questions:

In the light of the church's task as set forth in the objectives, and knowing what our youth situation is, what is the church's task in youth work?

What is the scope of youth work?

What is the purpose of youth work?

What is the process of youth work?

What should be the setup for the youth program?

Gather the statements from the subcommittees, edit them, and, together with the general statement, have them put in the form of a chart (see below), duplicated, and ready for distribution in connection with answering the question, What are we accomplishing? and the preparation of the report *An Appraisal of Christian Education in Our Church.* The "objectives" chart is the report on *Our Objectives in Christian Education.*

Go back over the process you have used in considering and setting objectives, asking these questions in order to analyze and evaluate it:

To what degree were the following qualities in evidence during the study of objectives:

    Responsible participation?

    Thoughtful participation?

    Creativity?

    Insight?

    Consensus?

    Commitment?

In what ways did the groups seem to have the feeling of hammering out the objectives in a democratic fashion?

What evidence was there of a sense of "the community of faith" working to define the bases of its life and mission?

How practical do the groups feel the results are?

In what ways do the results provide a new sense of direction for the study?

OUR OBJECTIVES IN CHRISTIAN EDUCATION					
	The Church's Task	The Scope of Christian Education	The Purpose of Christian Education	The Process of Christian Education	The Setup for Christian Education
General Objectives					
Implications for the Congregation at Large					
Implications for the Family					
Implications for Children's Work					
Implications for Youth Work					
Implications for Adult Work					

8

ANSWERING THE QUESTION, "WHAT ARE WE ACCOMPLISHING?" AND PREPARING THE REPORT
AN APPRAISAL OF CHRISTIAN EDUCATION IN OUR CHURCH

Evaluation is the comparison of what is with what ought to be. The study has progressed to the point where basic evaluation is possible, since objectives have been worked out for each area, and the situation in each area described. Using the objectives as criteria, each area of the Christian education program may be weighed, and intelligent and detailed judgments made about it.

Procedures

Have the members of the Committee on Evaluation and the members of the subcommittees review the two major reports produced thus far: *Facts on Christian Education in Our Church*, and *Our Objectives in Christian Education*.

Hold simultaneous consultations for appraisal, as follows:

A consultation of the Committee on Evaluation with representatives of the congregation and community.

A consultation of the subcommittee on Christian education in the congregation at large with representatives of the congregation and the community.

A consultation of the subcommittee on family life with representatives of the congregation.

A consultation of the subcommittee on children's work with representatives of the children's work groups.

A consultation of the subcommittee on youth work with representatives of the youth work groups.

A consultation of the subcommittee on adult work with representatives of the adult work groups.

Each consultation should follow this agenda:

1. Read and discuss each item in the appropriate section of *Facts on Christian Education in Our Church*.
2. Read and discuss each item in the appropriate section of *Our Objectives in Christian Education*.
3. Ponder the facts in the light of the objectives, comparing the appropriate section of *Facts on Christian Education in Our Church* with the corresponding section of *Our Objectives in Christian Education*.
   a. Note and list elements that seem to fulfill the objectives. (Record them on Form I, question 1.)
   b. Note and list elements that seem only partially to fulfill the objectives. (Record them on Form I, question 2.)
   c. Note and list elements that seem clearly to be working against the objectives. (Record them on Form I, question 3.)
   d. Note and list things that seem to be implied by the objectives that are not now a part of the situation and program. (Record them on Form I, question 4.)
4. Submit the findings of Form I to the Committee on Evaluation.

Edit the findings of Form I, the Committee on Evaluation having responsibility for the editorial work. Prepare the findings in the form of the report *An Appraisal of Christian Education in Our Church*, using the format of Form I.

Distribute *An Appraisal of Christian Education in Our Church* to all teachers, leaders, and others involved in leadership and administration. Offer it to any members of the congregation who are interested in studying it. Ask that reactions and suggestions be submitted to the Committee on Evaluation.

Analyze and evaluate the procedures used in appraising the Christian education program:

In what ways has the quality of participation in the study improved or deteriorated during the appraisal?

What evidence is there that *Facts on Christian Education in Our Church* and *Our Objectives in Christian Education* were faithfully and fully utilized?

To what extent has objectivity been maintained in the appraisal?

To what extent is there a sense among those involved that the appraisal has provided a sound and thorough base from which to plan for the future?

9

ANSWERING THE QUESTION,
"WHAT, THEN, DO WE NEED?"

Evaluation is not complete unless plans for the future are made that take account of the present situation in the light of the objectives. Having arrived at such an appraisal, the study concludes with planning for the future.

First, standards that are specifically applicable to the local situation are to be developed.

Standards should be arrived at co-operatively. This means that no prefabricated set of standards, regardless of its source, may be successfully applied in any local situation without adjustment and adaptation. This also means that the best people to build a standard are the people who are going to use it, providing they know their objectives, have the facts on their situation, and have submitted to the discipline of objective appraisal.

Standards represent specific aspects of the objectives applicable to the local situation and to the task at hand. They should be attainable, cover the whole program, provide a general plan for the program, and act as a basis for identifying needs and deciding on improvements. They should be carefully restudied and changed as the situation and needs change.

The identification of needs is the second step in constructive planning following the appraisal. Having developed standards, the study now proceeds to pin-point particular problems that require action if improvement is to be made. The development of standards and the identification of needs go hand in hand.

Procedures

Hold a conference of leaders and officers of the various groups in the Christian education program of the church (church school departments, family life groups, groups of adults, officers and advisers of youth groups, etc.), in which these groups will be helped to devise specific standards for their work in accordance with the study's findings, and move from the formulation of standards to the identification of their major needs.

This conference might take the form of a retreat or workshop, for a weekend or for several evenings, dealing with the questions, "What are we accomplishing?" and "What next steps shall we take?"

The devising of standards and identifying of needs may be accomplished in nine steps:

1. Ask the persons participating in the conference to familiarize themselves with:

   Basic documents on objectives: *The Objectives of Christian Education, The Objective of Christian Education for Senior High Young People,* and your denominational statement of objectives.

   The reports produced thus far in this study: *Facts on Christian Education in Our Church, Our Objectives in Christian Education,* and *An Appraisal of Christian Education in Our Church.*

2. Present to the entire group the major points in these materials, and have them thoroughly discussed. If the group is large, break frequently into small discussion units.

3. Divide into groups (members of church school departments, youth groups, etc.) to fill out Form J, Column B.

4. Have Form J, Column B, submitted, when completed, from each group to the Committee on Evaluation.

5. Have the Committee on Evaluation, or the conference as a whole:
   a. Study the findings of Form J, Column B, applying to them such critical questions as:

- Do they cover the area of the group's responsibility?
- Do they "add up"? Taken as a whole, do they represent a comprehensive set of standards for the church's program of Christian education?
- Are they consistent? Do the various sets of standards show a clear direction for the program, with substantial agreement on policy and procedure? Or do they show up basic disagreements that need to be discussed?
- Are they realistic?

b. Formulate suggestions and recommendations for changing or developing each set of standards that requires it.

c. Return copies of the standards to the groups that produced the standards, with the appropriate suggestions or recommendations. Request that the groups give consideration to these suggestions and do further work on the standards, if needed.

6. Divide the conference into the same groups as before, in order to take the next step: identifying the most pressing needs that are not being met.

a. Ask the group to review Section VII of *Facts on Christian Education in Our Church,* and questions 2, 3, and 4 in *An Appraisal of Christian Education in Our Church.*

b. Have each group fill out Form J, Column C. With the standards before it, have the group "brain-storm" on the unmet needs that it ought to be concerned with, such as the following:

Serious and penetrating grasp of the Christian faith and its implications for life and action on the part of adults.

Ministering to a changing neighborhood.

Policy decisions on priorities in the Christian education program: Are Christian education activities of the congregation at large to receive first priority; family activities second; and children's, youth, and adult activities third?

Breaking away from traditional practices and patterns in order that the church may become a family-centered fellowship.

Serious action on the community's social problems: alcohol, health, race relations, unreached persons, indifference to problems of war, crime and delinquency, housing, intergroup relations, politics, etc.

Revamping the church's recreation program and facilities.

A new conception of, and policy on, "homework."

Action on encroachment of other community groups on Christian education's time; Christian education's encroachment on the home's time.

The exercising of Christian responsibility outside the institutional church.

More knowledge on the part of the church at large on the aims and activities of the Christian education program, in order that the members of the church may begin to be brought closer to it.

Evaluation of other aspects of the work of Christian education: individual Christian development, the teaching-learning process, etc.

Revitalizing of leaders who have lost their vision.

Teachers grasping the objectives of Christian education and making specific and meaningful use of them in planning for and carrying on their work.

c. Weigh these suggestions, organizing them into an intelligible pattern. This will result in the retention of some, the alteration of others, the elimination of those not considered major or pressing, and the addition of some newly thought-of ideas.

d. Check this revised listing of needs against the standards again, to be sure that it represents the most pertinent and comprehensive listing possible.

7. Have Form J, Column C, submitted from each group to the Committee on Evaluation.

8. Have the Committee on Evaluation, or the conference as a whole:

a. Study the findings of Form J, Column C, applying to them such critical questions as:
- Do they represent genuine needs?
- Are they major and pressing needs—the church's profound concerns?
- Do they represent the most significant needs the particular group could seek to meet?
- Are they deeply challenging?
- Do they begin to indicate a "program" for

the group, or at least a program direction?

- Are they the responsibilities of the group suggesting them?
- In what ways might the responsibility for meeting the need be shared with other groups?

b. Formulate suggestions and recommendations for changing or developing each list of needs that requires it.

c. Return copies of the lists to the groups that produced them, with the appropriate suggestions or recommendations. Request that they give consideration to these recommendations and do further work on the lists, if needed.

9. Analyze and evaluate the procedures used in developing standards and identifying needs:

a. How carefully planned and successful was the approach to each group in enlisting it in the development of its standards and identifying its needs?

b. How thoroughgoing was its study and use of the basic documents?

c. In what ways did it use processes of group study and discussion designed to produce creative and acceptable results? How satisfactorily have the various members of the groups entered into the process of digging out the possibilities and unfulfilled responsibilities of the church's Christian education task?

d. What evidence is there that the standards are sound and practical, and that they are accepted?

e. What evidence is there that the needs identified are comprehensive, pointedly realistic, and challenging?

f. To what degree does the list of needs comprise a pattern of the "task for the future" in the church?

g. How painstaking, creative, and fruitful was the consideration of the findings of the groups by the Committee on Evaluation, or by the conference as a whole?

h. What new ideas on objectives occurred to the Committee on Evaluation, or to the conference as a whole, in the process of studying and commenting on the work of the groups?

10

ANSWERING THE QUESTION, "WHAT NEXT STEPS SHALL WE TAKE?" AND PREPARING THE REPORT
A PLAN OF ACTION FOR CHRISTIAN EDUCATION IN OUR CHURCH

DECIDING on next steps is the concluding part of the evaluation study. Facts have been discovered, objectives outlined, the situation appraised, standards set, the needs identified. Decision on appropriate action is now in order.

Procedures

Continue the conference (or retreat or workshop) of leaders and officers, begun in connection with the previous part of the study. At this point, the groups are to hammer out proposals for action that will meet the most pressing needs that they have discovered. This may be accomplished in seven steps:

1. Have each group fill out those portions of Form J, Column D, that apply to its work:

   a. Each group organizes its list of needs into a logical and workable pattern, probably following the outline of Form J, Column A.

   b. For each need, or area of need, suggest an appropriate action (or alternatives for action) that might be taken to meet the need. These constitute the group's suggestions on ways in which improvement may be sought. For instance (using the miscellaneous and very incomplete list of needs on p. 46):

   > Set up courses of university caliber for adults.
   >
   > Request the church's governing body to lead in developing a strategy for ministering to the changing neighborhood.
   >
   > Request that policy decisions be recommended by the committee on Christian education to the church's governing body.
   >
   > Recommend to the committee on Christian education that a workshop or insti-

   > tute be held to explore the implications of becoming a family-centered church.
   >
   > Set up a committee to investigate, and lead in action on, the community's social problems, with the understanding that it will also suggest specific action to all appropriate groups.
   >
   > Establish a recreation center, properly equipped and adequately staffed, remodeling existing facilities or building new ones.
   >
   > Try out "homework" ideas consisting of: participating in church and community activities; sharing in the life of the family; exploring the Bible, other books, music, the arts, and the devotional life; and pursuing interesting and worth-while hobbies.

   c. Shape up these suggestions into proposals for action that seem to give promise of meeting the needs and of engaging the utmost creative energy on the part of the group and its members.

2. Have Form J, Column D, submitted from each group to the Committee on Evaluation, or to the conference as a whole.

3. Have the Committee on Evaluation, or the conference as a whole, study the proposals for action that come from the groups. Compare and weigh them until it is possible to shape up something of a comprehensive plan of action for improvement. This comprehensive plan of action will include many of the groups' proposals. Some of their proposals may, however, have to be discarded, postponed, changed, or combined with others. New proposals may occur to the committee at this point, and may be included.

4. Have the Committee on Evaluation prepare the comprehensive plan of action for publication and distribution in the form of a report entitled: *A Plan of Action for Christian Education in Our Church.*

5. Have the Committee on Evaluation forward the plan to the church's governing body, requesting that it be adopted and authorized to be distributed to all.

6. Using *A Plan of Action for Christian Education in Our Church* and the previous proposals of the groups as guides, have the Committee on Evaluation:

   a. Formulate specific recommendations for individuals, organizations, and groups. Use Form K for this purpose.

   b. Give these recommendations to the individuals, organizations, and groups involved, preferably in conferences and consultations where they may be fully discussed.

   c. Suggest at the same time that in handling the recommendations and acting on them, the church's Christian education groups give serious consideration to the proposal for "action research" embodied in Form L.

7. Analyze and evaluate the procedures used in formulating the plan of action to meet the church's Christian education needs:

   a. What degree of meaningful and satisfying participation has been achieved by the people involved in this step of the study?

   b. Have the action proposals, *A Plan of Action for Christian Education in Our Church,* and the recommendations followed a logical and obvious progression?

   c. In what ways does the "Plan for Action Research," embodied in Form L, provide a promising means for carrying through the recommendations?

   d. In what ways have the proposals, the "Plan," and the recommendations helped to crystallize purposes, mobilize effort, and create new vision?

   e. At what points is it probable that further training will be needed to provide a basis for putting the recommendations into action?

   f. What other follow-up is required?

11

ANALYZING AND WEIGHING THE EVALUATION EXPERIENCE

THERE IS A REAL value in looking back and evaluating the study of the church's program of Christian education. Not only will it help in planning for conservation of the results of the experience, it will also help in improving future attempts at similar study. Here are some of the questions to use and keep in mind:

- Has the aim of the evaluation been achieved: to gain an accurate picture of the program, and develop an adequate plan for the future?

- As by-products of the study, does the church have a deeper understanding and more creative concern for Christian education?

- What has been learned about the process of evaluation that may be put to permanent use?

- What group procedures of study and action have been discovered that may become a part of the church's way of handling problems?

- Has the study mobilized the efforts of the whole church to a significant degree?

- What indications are there from the evaluation experience of the types of training that are needed by the church's Christian education workers?

- What further use is to be made of the four basic documents produced in the study:
  Facts on Christian Education in Our Church
  Our Objectives in Christian Education
  An Appraisal of Christian Education in Our Church
  A Plan of Action for Christian Education in Our Church

- What plan is there for the periodic revision of these documents, and for the renewal or continuance of evaluation of the program?

BIBLIOGRAPHY

The following materials are used so frequently in the evaluation study that they may be considered to be required:

The Objectives of Christian Education. National Council of Churches, 1958.

The Objective of Christian Education for Senior High Young People. National Council of Churches, 1958.

Denominational statements of the objectives of Christian education. Denominational standards and check lists for Christian education.

The following, while not required, will be found very useful in the study:

Douglass, Paul F., *The Group Workshop Way in the Church.* Association Press, 1956. A source of rich insights for this study, since it explores in great detail a process very similar to that suggested for evaluation of the church's Christian education program.

Gable, Lee J., *Christian Nurture Through the Church.* National Council of Churches, 1955. A standard work on the administration of Christian education in the parish.

Vieth, Paul H., *The Church School.* Christian Education Press, 1957. One of the most thorough and competent treatments of the problems of the organization, administration, and supervision of Christian education in the local church.

Part Three
FORMS

BASIC INFORMATION

To be used by the committee in consultation with others

I. General

1. Name of church:

2. Location:

3. National, regional, and local denominational connections:

II. History

4. Provide a brief sketch of the church's history: its beginnings; major developments and changes; their relation to wider movements of social change in the community and the world at large (for instance: wars, depressions, westward migration, suburban development, etc.); outstanding events; outstanding personalities.

5. Provide a brief historical picture of the development of Christian education in the church: its beginnings; major developments and changes; their relation to wider movements of social change in the community and world at large; outstanding events; outstanding personalities.

III. The Church's Community

6. Give a brief "impression" of the church's community, touching on its history; its topography; its socioeconomic situation, composition of the population (nationality, race, religion), population trends, business and industry; its educational resources; its character-building and recreational agencies; its social life; its health facilities; its social problems; its political situations; its civic, service, and labor organizations; and any other features of its life that create special opportunities or problems.

7. Describe the church's immediate neighborhood.

8. How has the community situation affected the church's Christian education program? How is it influencing it at present?

9. How is the church "seeking to meet the challenge of its community"?

IV. Membership

10. Total communicant membership, each year for the last fifteen years:

Year	Membership	Year	Membership	Year	Membership

11. Total active constituency at present (including active members and active nonmembers):

12. Constituency (including active members and active nonmembers):

       Within a half mile of the church:
       From a half mile to one mile from the church:
       Over one mile from the church:

(A spot map may be prepared, based on these data, for the "facts" report.)

13. Constituency (including active members and active nonmembers):

       Under 5 years of age:
       5-11 years of age:
       12-17 years of age:
       18-23 years of age:
       24-40 years of age:
       41-65 years of age:
       Over 65 years of age:

(A "population pyramid" based on these data may be prepared for the "facts" report.)

14. What approaches are used in bringing in new people?

15. How are persons transferred to the other churches?

V. Grouping and Grading

16. How are program groups set up and graded (by age, sex, etc.)?

17. How are persons placed in the various groups?

18. How do you decide to set up new groups?

19. How do you merge or disband program groups?

VI. Curriculum

20. How does the church select program resources and curriculum materials for the various program groups?

21. What program resources and curriculum materials are approved or recommended for use in the various program groups? (This applies to the overall program and curriculum plan, not to specific curriculum items.)

    a. What are their aims?

    b. How are they set up to achieve their aims?

    c. What methods do they employ?

    d. What basic experiences and materials (ideas and themes) do they cover?

22. What plan of curriculum co-ordination is in effect in the church? (How is unified curriculum planning done?)

VII. Leadership

23. How does the church enlist Christian education workers?

24. How does the church train and develop Christian education workers?

25. How many persons are there in the congregation who were Christian education workers at one time but are no longer active? What kinds of responsibilities did they have as Christian education workers?

VIII. Library Resources

26. What resources (books, audio-visual materials, etc.) are available?

27. How is their distribution and use managed?

IX. Co-operative Enterprises

28. How do the church and its leaders participate in the Christian education activities of the denomination?

29. How do the church and its leaders participate in interchurch councils and interchurch activities?

30. How does the church co-operate with secular community enterprises (schools, Red Cross, Community Chest, etc.)?

31. How does the church co-operate with local character-building and recreational agencies (Scouts, the Y, community centers, canteens)?

32. How does the church participate in co-operative leadership education?

33. How does the church participate in co-operative youth work?

X. Building and Equipment

34. Describe the grounds on which the church buildings are located.

35. What is the appraised value of the church property?

36. What is the plan for custodial care of the building?

37. How does the church handle the matter of repairs and replacements?

38. Draw a floor plan of the space used for Christian education. Give the over-all dimensions, and the dimensions of each room. List the permanent equipment in each room. Give the day and hour for each activity for each room.

XI. Finance

39. What is the church's total budget?

>   Current expenses:
>   Special receipts:
>   Benevolences:

40. What is the budget plan (manner of budgeting, supporting, and securing income) for the Christian education program as a whole?

41. Itemize the budget for Christian education:

42. Give the total Christian education budget each year for the last fifteen years:

Year	Budget	Year	Budget	Year	Budget

43. If a pledge system is used, what is the number of pledges?

How many participants do not pledge?

Number of pledges of:

>   Less than 10¢ per week:
>   10¢ to 24¢ per week:
>   25¢ to 49¢ per week:
>   50¢ to 99¢ per week:
> $1.00 to $2.49 per week:
> $2.50 or more per week:

Number of pledges from persons:

>   Under 5 years of age:
>   5-11 years of age:
>   12-17 years of age:
>   18-23 years of age:
>   24-40 years of age:
>   41-65 years of age:
>   Over 65 years of age:

XII. Records and Reports

44. What kinds of records (membership, attendance, activities, etc.) are kept?

45. How are the records used?

46. What system of reporting is used within the Christian education program?

47. What system is used for Christian education reports to the church?

XIII. Evaluation

48. How is individual growth and development evaluated?

49. How is group effectiveness evaluated?

50. How are leader-group relationships evaluated?

51. How is the program as a whole evaluated?

XIV. Interpretation of the Program

52. How is the program interpreted to the members themselves?

53. How is the program interpreted to the church?

54. How is the program interpreted to the public?

XV. Outreach

55. In what ways are participants being trained to take creative responsibility as Christians in the home, community, church at large, and the world?

56. In what ways are ecumenical appreciations, attitudes, and support being fostered in the individual and the group?

XVI. Organization and Co-ordination

57. Diagram the entire Christian education program, showing the relation of each group to the over-all program, and the lines of responsibility and authority now in operation.

58. Names of persons and groups participating in filling out this report:

ANALYSIS OF A GROUP AND ITS ACTIVITIES

To be used by officers and/or leaders of each group

I. General

1. Name of group (designation of committee, department, class, club, fellowship, choir, organization, etc.):

2. The group is responsible to (name of parent body, supervisory body, or administrator):

3. The group's stated or assumed purpose(s):

II. Membership

4. How does one become a member of the group?

5. Composition of the membership:

    a. Number according to residency:

        Within half a mile of the church:
        From a half mile to one mile from the church:

    b. Number according to sex:

        Male:
        Female:

    c. Number according to education:

        With a grade school education or less:
        With a high school education:
        With a college education:
        Who have done graduate work:

    d. Number according to marital status:

        Single:
        Married:
        Widowed:
        Divorced:

    e. Number according to employment classification:

        Public service:
        Domestic and personal service:
        Professional service:
        Clerical occupations:
        Students:

Executives, managers, etc.:
Skilled workers:
Unskilled workers:
Artists and journalists:
Housewives:
Unemployed:
Too young to be included in the above classifications:

f. Number according to church affiliation:

Church families:
Nonchurch families:

6. How long has the average member been connected with the group?

7. What is the average attendance as compared with the enrollment?

8. What parts do members of the group customarily take in its activities?

9. How are prospective members approached?

III. Leadership

10. Name each leader in the group and list his responsibilities.

11. What training have the leaders had for their work?

12. What is the average length of service for the leaders in the group?

13. What former positions in the Christian education program have the leaders held?

IV. Activities and Program

14. What is the group's annual program?

15. How is the program worked out in terms of quarterly, monthly, weekly, etc., activities?

16. How are seasonal emphases (holidays, etc.) used in the program?

17. Describe the highlights of a typical week in the life of the group.

V. Program Resources and Curriculum Materials

18. What program resources and curriculum materials are used?

19. How do you adapt them?

VI. Outreach

20. In what ways does the group train its members to take creative responsibility for witness, service, and social action outside?

21. In what ways does the group foster ecumenical appreciations, attitudes, and support?

VII. Place of Meeting

22. Describe your place of meeting. What are its good features? What are its bad features?

VIII. Finances

23. How is the group's work financed?

24. In what ways does the group co-operate in the total financial program of the church?

25. How are financial needs and challenges presented to the group and decided on by them?

IX. Condition of the Group

26. In what ways are the participants succeeding or failing in terms of the group's aims?

27. How is the morale of the group?

28. What are the major problems facing the group in its program and activities?

X. Records and Reports

29. What records of group life and activity are kept?

30. What use is made of the records?

31. What reports are made?

32. Who makes the reports?

33.   To whom are the reports made?

34. Name(s) and position(s) of person(s) making this report:

TEACHERS, LEADERS, AND ADMINISTRATORS

To be used by individual leaders

I. Personal Information

1. Name:

2. Position:

    a. In what capacity are you now serving?
    b. How long have you served in this capacity?
    c. What other positions do you know hold in the church?
    d. What former positions have you held in the church?

3. Church background:

    a. How long have you been a member of this church?
    b. In what other churches have you been active?

4. Vocation:

    a. What is your vocation at present?
    b. In what other lines of vocation have you engaged before?

5. Educational background:

    a. What schools have you attended?
    b. If you attended college, what was your major?
    c. If you have had graduate work, in what field?

6. Home:

    a. Who are the other members of your family?
    b. How much "waking time" do you average at home each week?
    c. What are your major activities at home?

7. What background and training have you had for your Christian education work?

8. Which of the books that you own and the periodicals that you take (exclusive of official curriculum and program materials) have been most useful to you?

9. What are your hopes or plans for service in Christian education in the future?

10. What personal values do you gain from participating in this work with other Christian leaders?

II. Information on Your Work

11. What purpose(s) do you have in your Christian education work?

12. What are your duties in the program?

13. What sort of weekly schedule do you use in fulfilling your duties (studying, planning, evaluating, leading, conducting informal group activities, attending meetings, consulting, visiting, approaching prospective members, devotional life, etc.)?

14. What steps do you take to understand the home and school (or working) life of those with whom you deal?

15. What do you see as the most pressing needs of those with whom you deal?

16. What program resources and curriculum materials do you use?

17. How do you adapt them?

18. What use do you make of library resources (books, audio-visual materials, etc.) in your work?

19. Describe a typical session(s) of the group(s) for which you are responsible. (Administrators will describe workers' conferences, committee sessions, supervisory conferences, etc.)

20. What methods do you customarily use in your work?

21. How do you handle conflicts, difficulties, and disturbances?

22. What do you do about irregularities of attendance, failure to follow through on responsibilities, etc.?

23. Describe your place of meeting. What are its good features? What would you like to see changed?

24. What parts do members of the group customarily take in its meetings and affairs?

25. How do you feel you are doing at your job?

26. In what ways are your participants succeeding or failing, in terms of your group's purposes?

27. How is the morale of the group?

28. What are the major problems you are facing in this work?

29. Records and reports:

    a. What records do you keep?
    b. What use do you make of them?
    c. What reports do you make? To whom?

30. How do you tell those you deal with, the church, and the public about your work?

31. What do you do to keep your group actively in touch with what is going on in the rest of the Christian education program?

32. How do you try to use the following in shaping your program?

    a. The individual member and his needs:
    b. The church, its heritage and mission:
    c. The community, its resources and needs:
    d. The world's needs and problems in our time:

33. What help do you receive in evaluating and improving your work? From whom?

34. In what ways other than this work do you feel that you express your Christian faith and sense of Christian calling?

OBSERVATION OF A GROUP

To be used by designated observers

During the evaluation, needed insights may be gained by having observers visit various groups, departments, classes, committees, and the like. This form is provided to guide these observers in the approaches to use, the observations to make, and the kinds of information that may be most usefully reported to the committee and subcommittees. (In many cases regular members of a group may well act as observers.)

To the observer:

You will be given certain assignments, by the committee or by a subcommittee, of groups to be visited in the course of the evaluation. Arrangements will be cleared ahead of time, but you should check personally a few days ahead of time with the leader or group to be visited.

Secure and study the program resources and curriculum materials to be used, or (in the case of a committee meeting) familiarize yourself with the proposed agenda.

Arrive well ahead of the arrival of the first participants.

Be seated in an inconspicuous place, but one from which you will be able to see the proceedings. (If, during the visit, the group changes its location, change with them, but again seek an inconspicuous place from which to observe.)

If the leader wishes to introduce you to the group, acknowledge the introduction very briefly, indicating your pleasure at being their guest on behalf of the study. Take no other part in the session.

Take notes from the time you arrive, throughout the session, until the group has departed, using the first part of the form below. Fill out the second part of the form after you have had a chance to let the meaning of the observation "sink in" a while. Let the questions in Part 2 help you in knowing what to observe.

Stay with the same group for the entire session. Never skip from group to group.

If you are visiting a group of small children, some may engage you in conversation or ask for help. Respond quietly, as a courteous adult, but get back to your note-taking as soon as possible. If necessary, explain to them that you are busy.

If you have a chance after the session, ask the leader some of the questions you have jotted down in the right-hand column of your notes. Questions designed to get further factual information are appropriate;

questions of a critical or judgmental character are not appropriate.

Be careful in talking with the leader or group (never during the session period) to avoid any suggestions of criticism. Your purpose is to find out what is taking place, the methods and procedures being used, and the purposes involved.

As you depart, thank the leader and tell him that when your notes are written up they will be turned over to the appropriate committee to assist them in the study.

Observation Record, Part 1 (to be filled out during the visit).

Designation of group observed:

Place:

Date:

Name of leader(s):

Background data on group (enrollment, activities leading up to session observed, etc.):

Description of meeting place:

Time	(In this column, keep a factual account of what goes on in the session: activities, pupil response, problems arising, etc.)	(In this column, record your comment and questions on what you are seeing and hearing.)

<u>Observation Record, Part 2 (to be filled out after the visit)</u>.

Comment rather fully on the following items, in a way that will provide the committee or subcommittee with insight into the session of the group that you visited:

I. <u>General</u>

1. The purpose(s) of the session:

2. The relation of what went on in this session to the total task of the church in Christian education:

II. <u>Activities</u> <u>and</u> <u>Program</u>

3. How is the group organized to do its work?

4. How was the session prepared for, by the leader(s) and the group members?

5. How did the pre-session activities relate to the group's purpose(s)?

6. What varieties of activities were engaged in during the session?

7. How was the work individualized by the leader(s) and the group, related to the abilities, needs, and interests of each member?

8. How was the session made to hold together?

9. What new ideas, attitudes, skills, and challenges seemed to develop?

10. What was the role of worship in the session?

11. What possibilities of follow-up developed?

12. What next steps were indicated?

III. <u>Curriculum</u> <u>and</u> <u>Program</u> <u>Resources</u>

13. What curriculum and program resources were used?

14. What subject matter was dealt with?

15. How were curriculum and program resources planned for, used, and adapted?

16. In what ways did they seem to be suitable or unsuitable?

IV. <u>Leadership</u> <u>and</u> <u>Membership</u>

17. What abilities, interests, and needs were evident in the members?

18. How were they used?

19. How did the leader and group proceed with the session?

20. What varieties of approaches were evident?

21. What leadership and membership roles were assumed?

22. What was done to guide the group's thought and work?

23. What was done to get the subject matter across?

24. What was done to individualize the session?

25. What degree of individual participation was achieved?

26. What degree of personal responsibility was achieved?

27. What awareness did the leader and members seem to have of the significance of the personal interaction that was going on among them?

V. Condition of the Group

28. Characterize the atmosphere, degree of purposefulness, and morale of the group.

29. What major problems were evident in this group?

30. Name of observer:

PARTICIPANTS' QUESTIONNAIRE

To be used by individual participants, or designated
persons interviewing individual participants

Some of the people who participate in the church's Christian education
program have been selected to help with the study and evaluation of the program. You are one of the persons who have been selected. Please do two
things: Tell about your part in one of the sessions of a group you belong
to, and answer the questions at the end of the form.

Fill out this form, telling about your part in the session of

_____   _____
(Name of group)   (Date)

_____   _____
(Your name)   (Name of interviewer - if any)

Time	Activity	What I Did	With Whom

Answer these questions about the session:

1. What were your personal reactions to the session?
2. What did you contribute to it?
3. What did you get from it?
4. In what ways do you think it achieved, or did not achieve, its
   purpose?
5. How do you think it could have been improved?

Note: This form may be filled out personally by participants from junior
         age and up, including adults. It may be used in connection with
         any type of group session, including classes, clubs, committee
         meetings, etc. When it is used with children of primary age or
         younger, an interviewer should fill out the first section; and in-
         stead of the questions in the second section, the child may be
         asked simply for his reaction to his part in the session: "How
         did you feel about what you did? What did you think of it?"

PARENTS' QUESTIONNAIRE

To be used by parents of individual participants

In connection with the study and evaluation of the church's Christian education program, a few selected parents of children and youth participating in the program are being asked to answer this questionnaire. The questionnaire is designed to provide information on the ways in which the home and church are now working together in Christian education, or failing to do so. You are among the parents selected. Please answer the questions below as candidly as possible.

I. Personal Information

1. Names (husband and wife):

2. Address:

3. Names and ages of children:

4. Business or occupation:

5. How long have you been connected with this church?

6. In what capacities have members of the family served in the church's work?

7. What activities do members of the family engage in and enjoy at home?

8. Chief interests of members of the family, outside the home and church:

II. Information on the Program

9. What are the major ways in which you, as parents, have co-operated with the church's Christian education program?

10. When, and in what way, did you first become interested as parents in the Christian education program?

11. How do you feel that the carry-over from the church's program of Christian education to your home has been effective?

12. How do you feel that it has been ineffective?

13. What evidences of Christian growth and development have you noticed in the members of your family?

14. What objectives, ideas, and plans do you have for the Christian education of the members of your family?

15. How aware do you think the church is of these objectives, ideas, and plans of yours?

16. What problems do you face in the Christian education of the members of your family?

17. How aware do you think the church is of these problems?

18. What suggestions do you have for the church's assisting you more effectively in the Christian education of the members of your family?

19. How much of the initiative in the relation of home and church comes from the church, and how much from you as parents?

20. In what ways has the church helped you to understand your role as Christian parents?

CHRISTIAN EDUCATION IN THE FAMILY

To be used by the subcommittee on family life
in consultation with others

I. Basic Information

1. Types of families in the church:

   a. Number of adult households:
   b. Number of young families:
   c. Number of three-generation families:
   d. Number of single adults who maintain a home:
   e. Number of non-normal families and broken homes:
       Describe the kinds of situations involved in these non-normal and
       broken homes:
   f. Others:
       Explain:

2. Households in various stages of family growth:

   a. Number of newly married couples:
   b. Number of families with their first baby:
   c. Number of families with children:
   d. Number of families with adolescents:
   e. Number of "retired" parents with married children:

3. What is the trend in the community's birth rate?

4. Family mobility:

   a. Are families moving into the community?
       In what numbers?
       What are their characteristics?

   b. Are families moving into the neighborhood of the church?
       In what numbers?
       What are their characteristics?

   c. Are families moving out of the community?
       In what numbers?

   d. Are families moving out of the neighborhood of the church?
       In what numbers?

II. The General Program

5. Who is responsible for the church's ministry to families?

6. How are the needs, concerns, and interests of the church's families
    ascertained?

7. In what ways does the family life program seek to strengthen the family itself as a generating center of Christian life for all its members?

8. What procedures are used for the development of home-church co-operation?

9. What use is made of parent-teacher meetings; neighborhood parents' meetings; parents' classes; class parents or sponsors; open house in church school, with interpretation of program to parents; provision of suggestions and materials for family observation of church holidays and festivals; church family nights; visitation of families in the home; use of calendar to suggest family activities and recommend books; provision of magazines and pamphlets; library resources; Sunday morning family services; family camping, etc.?

10. What is done to encourage Christian education activities in homes without children?

11. In what ways does the church's family life program recognize and deal with the stages of family growth?

12. What use is made of denominational curriculum, literature, and leadership in the family life program?

13. How is the church's family life program related to the rest of the church's program?

III. Preparation for Marriage

14. Describe in detail your Christian education program concerning preparation for marriage. Indicate the age levels and groups in which consideration is given to the following topics: youth-parent relationships and adjustments, boy-girl relationships, reproduction and physiology, the psychology of sex, marriage, and parenthood as Christian vocation.

IV. Premarital Counseling

15. What has been the minister's preparation for premarital counseling?

16. What procedures does he use?

17. What materials does he provide and/or recommend to couples?

18. What instruction is given, other than by the minister?

19. In what ways is premarital counseling followed up by the church after marriage?

V. Family Guidance

20. What help is given in interpreting Christian education to the families of the church (its purpose, resources, methods, and the functions of the home in carrying it forward)?

21. Describe the provision made by the church for the consideration of psychological preparation for parenthood, the role of the child in the family, the care and development of babies and children, interpretation of the religious experience of the child at various age levels, development of a sense of responsibility in children, child psychology, sibling relationships, and other common problems.

22. What reading materials are available to parents when specifically needed?

23. What provision is there for counseling on marital adjustment, the wife's career, budgeting of family time, budgeting of family income, getting along with neighbors (interfaith, interracial relationships, etc.), progressive orientation of children with parents to life's changes (going to school, first time away from home, military service, in-law relationships, etc.)?

24. What provision is there for counseling of parents with handicapped or disturbed children?

25. What kinds of lay counseling are available in the church?

VI. Utilizing Community Resources

26. What resources for family life and family guidance are available in the community (in connection with the public schools, health clinics, YMCA and YWCA, child guidance clinics, Legal Aid, etc.)?

27. Describe the ways the church makes use of these community resources.

28. What information as to community resources are home visitors given?

29. How are the facilities and resources of the denomination and councils of churches used in the family life program?

30. How does the church participate in and support various aspects of the community's family life program?

31. Names of persons filling out this report:

(Adapted from a survey conducted in the churches of New York City by the Departments of Religious Education of New York University and Union Theological Seminary, the Protestant Council of the City of New York, and the Social Hygiene Division of the New York Tuberculosis and Health Association.)

OBJECTIVES

To be used by the committee and its subcommittee
in consultation with others

This form is designed to assist in thinking through, adapting, and making specific adaptations of the objectives of Christian education. Five areas are considered:

The church's task
The scope of Christian education
The purpose of Christian education
The process of Christian education
The way Christian education, as a program, is to be set up

The Committee on Evaluation is to work out a general statement of objectives that will be useful and applicable to the local situation. The statement is to cover all five areas, and is to be worked out using this form.

Then each of the subcommittees (Christian education in the congregation at large, family life, children's work, youth work, and adult work) is to formulate a statement of the implications of the general statement for the area of the subcommittee's concern.

1. What is the church's task?

   a. Consider the following statement about the church and its task: The context of Christian education is the church, the worshiping, witnessing, working community of Christ's followers. "The mission of the church is to witness to the good news of God's redeeming love as revealed in the life, death, and resurrection of Jesus Christ; to hold out a continuing summons to the worship and service of God; to maintain and extend a fellowship in which persons, led by the Holy Spirit, may respond in faith to his transforming power; to help persons, both as individuals and in society, to develop such attitudes and relationships with God and one another as will lead to an increasing Christian witness through Christian life and service to human need, and to pray in word and deed 'thy Kingdom come.'" (The Objectives of Christian Education, p. 18.)

   b. How could the ideas in this statement be accepted, changed, added to, dropped, or rephrased so as to constitute a useful and meaningful statement of the context of Christian education for your church?

2. What is the scope of Christian education's concern?

   a. Consider the following statement about the concerns of Christian education:

The scope of Christian education is the whole field of relationships (God, man, nature, and history) in the light of the
gospel. The whole field of relationships, seen in the light of the
gospel, may be viewed as follows:

God (Father, Son, and Holy Spirit) comes to man in the
Word, made known to us in the Bible and in the life of the
church, calling us into relationship with him and thus
throwing the light we need on:
Man - so that we see and relate to him as he was created
(in the image of God), as he is (sinner), and as he may become (redeemed):
        as self,
        in common human relations,
        as creator, possessor, and transmitter of the
            culture and heritage;
Nature - so that we see and relate to it as the setting in
which God has created man to live;
History - so that we see and relate to it as the continuum
of God's activity and man's life.
(Wyckoff, Theory and Design of Christian
Education Curriculum, p. 125.)

b. How could the ideas in this statement be accepted, changed, added
to, dropped, or rephrased so as to constitute a true and useful
statement of the scope of Christian education for your church!

3. What is the purpose of Christian education?

a. Consider the following statement of the purpose of Christian education:

"The objective of Christian education is to help persons to be
aware of God's self-disclosure and seeking love in Jesus Christ
and to respond in faith and love - to the end that they may
know who they are and what their human situation means, grow as
sons of God rooted in the Christian community, live in the
Spirit of God in every relationship, fulfill their common discipleship in the world, and abide in the Christian hope."
(The Objective of Christian Education for Senior High Young
People, pp. 14-15.)

b. How could the ideas in this statement be accepted, changed, added
to, dropped, or rephrased so as to constitute a true and useful
statement of the purpose of Christian education for your church?

4. What is the process of Christian education?

a. Consider the following:

77

A statement of the process of Christian education as participation in the life and work of the witnessing community:

> The method of Christian education is participation (or involvement, or engagement) in the life the church lives and the work it does, through: study (of the Bible, history, Christian thought, and contemporary affairs), creative expression (through music, the spoken word, and the other arts), action (witness, service, and social action), fellowship (group living and outreach), stewardship, and worship.

A statement of the process of Christian education as the undertaking of learning tasks:

> "Christian education engages the person in certain learning tasks. Throughout his life he is required to listen with growing alertness to the gospel and respond to it in faith and love as he undertakes the tasks of exploring the whole field of relationships in light of the gospel, discovers meaning and value in light of the gospel, appropriating that meaning and value personally, and assuming personal and social responsibility in light of the gospel." (The Objective of Christian Education for Senior High Young People, p. 15.)

b. How could the ideas in these statements be accepted, changed, added to, dropped, or rephrased so as to constitute a meaningful and useful statement of the process of Christian education for your church?

5. How shall the Christian education program be set up?

a. Consider the following statements about the curriculum (curriculum-program) and administration (organization, management, and supervision) of Christian education:

The curriculum (curriculum-program) of Christian education must be so designed and built that it:

> Uses the process of Christian education.
> Deals adequately with the scope of Christian education.
> Gives promise of accomplishing the purpose of Christian education.

The administration (organization, management, and supervision) of Christian education must be so designed and built that it:

> Is a true expression of the church working at its task.
> Covers every aspect of the scope of Christian education.

b. How could the ideas in these statements be accepted, changed, added
    to, dropped, or rephrased so as to constitute a true and useful
    statement of the way Christian education should be set up in your
    church?

6. Names of persons filling in this form:

APPRAISAL

To be used by the committee and its subcommittees in
consultation with others

1. What elements in the situation and program seem to fulfill the ob-
    jectives?

2. What elements in the situation and program seem only partially to
    fulfill the objectives? (Specify the shortcomings in each case.)

3. What elements seem clearly to be working against the fulfillment of
    the objectives?

4. What things seem to be implied by the objectives that are not now a
    part of the situation and program?

5. Names of persons filling in this form:

FORMULATION OF STANDARDS, IDENTIFICATION OF NEEDS,
AND STEPS TOWARD IMPROVEMENT

To be used by Christian education
groups in the church

A standard is a specific goal that is sought in Christian education.
Standards, in turn, suggest needs. Needs call for appropriate action.
This form is designed to assist in getting at such goals for the various
groups in the church's program of Christian education, discovering the
needs that exist, and suggesting things that might be done to meet them as
needs arise and change.

Column A gives the major areas of concern and responsibility in the
program. Insert in Column B the standards that are appropriate for your
group in each area that applies to your work. List in Column C the needs
for improvement that are suggested by the standards. List in Column D the
steps that might be undertaken to meet the needs.

Observe the following principles in connection with the standards:

They should cover the whole area of the group's concern and responsibility.

They should be specifically related to problems and possibilities that have turned up in the "facts" and appraisal reports.

They should be specific outgrowths of the contents of the objectives chart.

Observe the following principles in connection with the needs:

They should correlate directly with the standards.

They should provide clues to "next steps" between the situation
as it is and the objectives.

They should be selective - major and pressing needs, not trivial
or inconsequential needs.

Observe the following principles in connection with the action proposals:

They should be genuine action proposals, suggesting things to be done.

They should grow directly out of the needs.

They should be held as proposals for the time being, until the Committee on Evaluation has had an opportunity to study the proposals
from each group and make recommendations to each group.

Name of group filling out this form:

Names of persons working in the group:

COLUMN A AREAS OF CONCERN	COLUMN B STANDARDS
I. Fundamental orientation	
1. The church's task. (Insert here your statement of the church's task from the first column of Our Objectives in Christian Education.)	
II. Curriculum and program	
2. Scope. (Insert here your statement of the scope of Christian education from the second column of Our Objectives in Christian Education.)	

COLUMN C NEEDS	COLUMN D ACTION PROPOSED TO MEET NEEDS

COLUMN A AREAS OF CONCERN	COLUMN B STANDARDS
II. Curriculum and program (cont'd)	
3. Purpose. (Insert here your statement of the purpose of Christian education from the third column of <u>Our Objectives in Christian Education</u>.)	
4. Process. (Insert here your statement of the process of Christian education from the fourth column of <u>Our Objectives in Christian Education</u>.)	

COLUMN C NEEDS	COLUMN D ACTION PROPOSED TO MEET NEEDS

COLUMN A AREAS OF CONCERN	COLUMN B STANDARDS
III. Administration (planning, organization, management, and supervision)	
5. Principles of administration. (Insert here your statement of the setup for Christian education from the fifth column of Our Objectives in Christian Education.)	
6. Lines of responsibility and authority: the tasks and patterns of relationships of the church's governing body, the committee on Christian education and its subcommittees, the Christian education groups (the church school, etc.), and the Christian education personnel (staff and officers).	

COLUMN C NEEDS	COLUMN D ACTION PROPOSED TO MEET NEEDS

COLUMN A AREAS OF CONCERN	COLUMN B STANDARDS
III. Administration (cont'd)	
7. Planning and setting up the program in terms of persons to be served and functions to be performed, the committee on Christian education being chiefly responsible.	
8. Christian education in the congregation at large (worship, functional committees, task groups, all-church events, etc.).	
9. Christian education in the home.	

COLUMN C NEEDS	COLUMN D ACTION PROPOSED TO MEET NEEDS

89

COLUMN A AREAS OF CONCERN	COLUMN B STANDARDS
III. Administration (cont'd)	
10. Children's work, youth work, and adult work in the congregation:	
a. The participants: Grouping (functional groups, age-level groups, permanent groups, changing groups, etc.). Membership (recruiting; outreach to various cultural, racial, economic, and age groups; orienting, regularizing, maintaining). Participation and response (in undertaking the learning tasks, in planning and setting goals, in working toward goals, in Christian vocation in the church and beyond, in personal study, in creative expression, in personal action, in fellowship, in stewardship, in worship and prayer, in preparing for church membership, in assuming the responsibilities of church membership, etc.).	

COLUMN C NEEDS	COLUMN D ACTION PROPOSED TO MEET NEEDS

91

COLUMN A AREAS OF CONCERN	COLUMN B STANDARDS
III. Administration (cont'd)	
10. Children's work, youth work, and adult work in the congregation (cont'd):	
b. The staff (including all-professional and nonprofessional): Selection, enlistment, and orientation. Provision of accurate job descriptions. Performance (in planning, in group participation, in leadership, in outreach, in evaluating and reporting, in personal study and growth, in creative expression, in personal action, in fellowship, in stewardship, in worship and prayer, in Christian vocation in the church and beyond, etc.). Training. Tenure. Fellowship.	

COLUMN C NEEDS	COLUMN D ACTION PROPOSED TO MEET NEEDS

COLUMN A AREAS OF CONCERN	COLUMN B STANDARDS
III. Administration (cont'd)	
10. Children's work, youth work, and adult work in the congregation (cont'd):	
c. Buildings, equipment, and supplies.	
d. Keeping and using records and reports.	
e. Financing (manner of budgeting, manner of securing income, sources of income, service and mission, etc.).	

COLUMN C NEEDS	COLUMN D ACTION PROPOSED TO MEET NEEDS

95

COLUMN A AREAS OF CONCERN	COLUMN B STANDARDS
III. Administration (cont'd)	
10. Children's work, youth work, and adult work in the congregation (cont'd):	
f. Scheduling (Sunday, week-end, weekday, vacations, summer).	
g. Co-ordination and communication: With the rest of the Christian education program (including the home). With the rest of the church's program. With community agencies. With the public (including public relations). With the denomination and inter-denominational councils.	
h. Operational services (audio-visual, library, etc.).	

COLUMN C NEEDS	COLUMN D ACTION PROPOSED TO MEET NEEDS

COLUMN A AREAS OF CONCERN	COLUMN B STANDARDS
III. Administration (cont'd)	
11. Co-operative community services (vacation church schools; week-day church schools, youth work; leadership education; radio, television, etc.; meeting human need in the community and beyond through social service; social action on community problems and political issues, etc.).	
12. Camps and conferences.	
13. Working out and applying standards.	
14. Evaluating (individual Christian development, the teaching-learning process, program and curriculum, Christian education in the congregation, Christian education in the home, etc.).	

COLUMN C NEEDS	COLUMN D ACTION PROPOSED TO MEET NEEDS

COLUMN A AREAS OF CONCERN	COLUMN B STANDARDS
III. Administration (cont'd)	
15. Improvement:	
a. Administrative relations.	
b. Curriculum and program.	
c. Group leadership (pre-service training, observation, workers' conferences, library service, on-the-job training, leadership schools, coaching conferences and previews, clinics, workships, etc.).	
IV. Other areas of concern	

COLUMN C NEEDS	COLUMN D ACTION PROPOSED TO MEET NEEDS

RECOMMENDATION

To be used by the committee and its subcommittees

To (designation of staff member, officer, organization, or group):

Subject (title of recommendation):

Recommendation:

Reasons for the recommendation:

Recommended for (check one):   Immediate action_____

Long-range planning_____

A PLAN FOR ACTION RESEARCH

To be used by individuals, organizations, and
groups acting on recommendations

The Christian educator who is puzzled and concerned about some aspect of his work tries hard to be as objective as he can as he goes about trying to improve the situation. Action research may be able to help him. The successful use of action research depends upon: the feeling of freedom to talk about difficulties; many opportunities for the development of creative ideas about new and presumably better ways of doing things - free and frank discussion among the staff, reading research literature, visiting other groups, examining new materials, and careful examination by the educator of his own past experience; a widespread feeling of support for trying out new ideas; careful attention to getting evidence or facts; provision of time and resources for experimentation - time to think, to plan, to gather and interpret data, to discover and create or bring together new resources needed for experimentation.

The following seven steps might be involved in action research in Christian education:

1. Define the problem:

2. Why does the problem exist?

3. What alternatives are there for solving the problem?

4. What are the arguments for and against each of the alternatives?

5. Which of the alternatives, then, shall be chosen to be tried out?

6. What is the evidence for and against the chosen solution, when it has been tried out?

7. What has been learned from the experience that should:

      Modify existing procedures?

      Apply to future situations?

(Suggested by the article "Action Research and the Classroom Teacher," by Stephen M. Corey, in the NEA Journal, February, 1954.)

How to Evaluate Your Christian Education Program

BY D. CAMPBELL WYCKOFF

This book provides a plan for surveying and appraising Christian education work in the local church. Going far deeper than the "check list" type of evaluation, it takes account of the best in recent thought in Christian education theory, and at the same time provides practical step-by-step guidance. The plan calls for the setting up of a committee on evaluation—a committee to include officers, teachers, group leaders, parents, pupils, group members, even "neighbors" in a study of the existing situation, setting objectives and standards, identifying needs, and deciding on action to meet these needs. The plan has been field-tested in more than two dozen churches of various denominations. Included are full-size sample forms suitable for duplication in quantities needed by the user of the manual. This is a Cooperative Publication Association text.

Dr. Wyckoff is Professor of Christian Education at Princeton Theological Seminary. He is the author of many books including *The Task of Christian Education, The Gospel and Christian Education,* and *Theory and Design of Christian Education Curriculum.*

THE WESTMINSTER PRESS

20-0387